68000 User Guide

Lionel Fleetwood

SIGMA PRESS

ISBN 1 85058 001 4

Published by:

SIGMA PRESS
5 Alton Road
Wilmslow
Cheshire UK.

Distributors:

UK, Europe, Africa:
JOHN WILEY & SONS LIMITED
Baffins Lane, Chichester
West Sussex, England.

Australia:
JOHN WILEY & SONS INC.
GPO Box 859, Brisbane
Queensland 40001, Australia.

Acknowledgments

MC68000, MC68000 and their derivatives are trade marks of Motorola Inc.

Printed and bound in Great Britain by
J. W. Arrowsmith Ltd., Bristol

INTRODUCTION

It is only ten years since the launch in 1974 of Motorola's M6800, a fast, cheap and reliable microprocessor which helped to bring computing power to places where it had never been before.

The M6800 gave rise to a family which included the 6801, 6802 and the all-purpose 6809 microcomputer, each of them superior in some way to its predecessor. But 8 bits gave way to 16, kilobytes of memory to megabytes, and prices of chips dropped from dollars to cents.

The MC68000 reflects this trend. With a 32-bit address bus, 32-bit data and address registers and a 4 to 12.5 MHz clock, the MC68000 has become a popular device and currently powers a host of computer systems including (in its 8-bit version) the Sinclair QL and the Apple Macintosh, as well as larger systems.

The demand for expertise in MC68000 machine language programmers will grow as the demand for the chip grows: exponentially. This book aims to impart a measure of that expertise.

CONTENTS

How to use this book

Assembly language programming is not particularly difficult, but it is a convoluted subject and it is difficult to absorb all the ideas simultaneously. On the other hand, it is difficult to understand the concepts in isolation from each other.

This book is divided into eleven sections and chapters, each of which deals with a group of topics. Each section has an introductory page which indicates the flavour of that section.

To give yourself an overview of the subject, go through the book and read these eleven introductions first. Then work through the book from front to back. If you have an assembler at your disposal, try to write simple segments of code using the features you learn at each stage.

No-one can claim that assembly is easy: but I believe this approach will make it as simple as possible - which, according to Einstein, is the simplest it is allowed to be.

SECTION 1
Finding Your Way Around the MC68000

This section contains:

1.1 A summary of MC68000 system architecture.

1.2 The programming model of the MC68000.

This section is to orient you. At the end of it you should have a clear idea of those parts of the MC68000 of interest to an assembly language programmer.

1.1 A summary of MC68000 system architecture.

A system based on the MC68000 consists of:

the processor:

which contains registers, symbol r:
8 data registers, symbols dO-d7 which may contain data as:
8-bit bytes,
16-bit words
32-bit long words

7 address registers, symbols aO-a6 which may contain addresses as:
16-bit words
32-bit long words

two stack pointers:
one for the supervisor, symbol sa7
one for the user, symbol ua7

one status register, symbol sr which has :
a system byte, symbol ssr which has :
an s-bit:
1 = supervisor mode
O = user mode
and a t-bit:
1 = trace on
O = trace off
an interrupt priority mask of 3 bits:I ,I ,I
and a user byte, symbol ccr
with a carry flag C
an extend flag X
an overflow flag V
a zero flag
and a negative flag N

one program counter, symbol pc
which points to the address of the next instruction

internal registers inaccessible to the programmer

a data bus which may be 8, 16, or 32 bits wide

an address bus which is 32 bits wide
    (but only the 68020 uses all 32 bits - the rest use 24)

some memory which may be up to 16 megabytes of
    random-access read/write memory (ram)
    random-access read-only memory (rom)

input-output ports which are memory-mapped

peripherals connected to the i/o ports or to memory by means
of direct memory access dma.

That's the hardware. This is the software:

system software including
    the monitor program
    the operating system
    assemblers
    interpreters
    compilers
    utilities
applications software - which you write

We will be dealing with the system from the point of view of the
assembly-language programmer, who must have an appreciation of
all parts of the system and the way in which they interact in order
to turn out programs which will do the job without molesting the
processor, offending the user, wrecking programs written by other
programmers or subverting the operating system.

1.2 The programming model of the MC68000.

The programming model of a microprocessor is a way of representing those parts which are of interest to the programmer. A BASIC or FORTRAN programming model is different from a machine code programming model, simply because a BASIC programmer 'sees' the machine differently. In BASIC, you don't need to know about stacks, registers and condition codes. If you do, you are suffering from incomplete documentation, or the implementation of Basic you are using is a poor one, or you're trying to do something which is better done in another language. Fig 1.1 shows you a programming model of the MC68000. This is how you must think of the machine if you are to write good code for it.

The elements of the MC68000 are:

* the processor
* the buses
* the registers
* the memory
* the stack pointers
* the program counter

Let's look at each of these separately.

1.2.1 The processor

The processor is the driving force behind a computer. Just as you may elect to ride a bicycle one day and drive a truck the next, the processor is hardly constrained as to the system it may actually drive. Because 16-bit processors are intermediate in price and performance between 8-bit and 32-bit devices, the MC68000 drives a lot of machines which can be classed as big micros or small minis and at least one small micro - the Sinclair QL.

The processor itself is no simple device, consisting of thousands of parts crammed into a very small area. It has certain functional areas which are aggregations of some of these smaller parts. Some of these you should be aware of:

* The instruction fetcher reads instructions and puts them into a buffer so that when the processor finishes executing one instruction, the next is waiting.

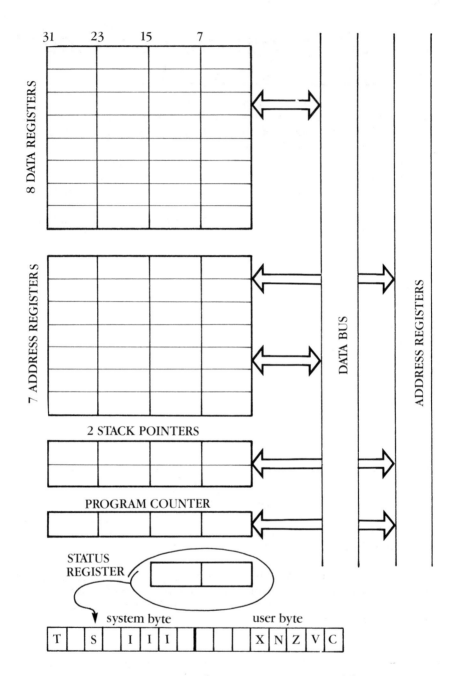

Figure 1.1 MC68000 Programming Model

* The instruction decoder turns an instruction into a set of internally executable commands. This is not the same as an assembler.
* The arithmetic logic unit performs arithmetic and logical operations.
* Internal registers not directly accessible to the programmer.

The processor's whole life is spent retrieving instructions which tell it either to get data from somewhere, pass data to somewhere or do something to the data. If you understand this not too complicated idea you will have a clear and valuable insight into the behaviour of any microprocessor. In order to shift data around, the processor needs two buses (which are simply electrical connectors) between various devices in the system. There are two different buses, one for data and one for addresses.

1.2.2 The buses

The address bus in any MC68000 system is 32 bits wide, but only 24 of these are actually used to carry an address (except in the 68020). This means that the MC68000 can address up to $2^{**}24$ bytes or 16 megabyte (16Mb) of data. Memory space is divided into supervisor and user program and data areas and, if these areas are kept separate externally, the MC68000 based systems can address 16Mb in each of them individually, giving a total memory space of 64Mb. The mechanics of this need not concern a novice programmer.

Addresses are put onto the address bus from the address registers. As you can see, these have access to the address bus and the data bus, whereas data registers have access to the data bus only. Since an address register has 32 bits it would seem that the MC68000 should be able to address up to 4 gigabytes, but, except for the 68020, its architecture does not presently allow for such a huge memory space - nor is it certain that there is anyone around who can afford that much memory. (Admittedly, there are Virtual Memory systems (with hard disks) that do use that much!)

The data bus can vary in width from 8 to 32 bits. The QL has an 8-bit data bus, which means that it takes four trips to fill a 32-bit data register. This is rather like training a sprinter and then chopping one of his legs off. A 32-bit data bus can carry a long word at one time, so that it can load a register in one trip. Systems with 32-bit data buses are naturally very fast at applications where a large amount of data has to be transferred to and from a large memory space. Such applications occur, for instance, in handling high-resolution full-colour display, so MC68000s are in favour for this type of work.

1.2.3 The Registers

A large part of a processor's work involves arithmetic and logical manipulation of data. This cannot be done unless the data is first brought into a storage device called a register, where it is manipulated before being restored to the device from which it came - usually memory. The MC68000 has five types of register:

* Data registers, each 32 bits wide
* Address registers, also 32 bits wide - one of which is used as the stack pointer
* Internal registers invisible to you
* The status register, 16 bits wide
* The program counter, 32 bits wide

There are 8 data registers and 8 address registers, but one of the address registers is duplicated, so that there are actually 17 32-bit registers available to the processor. Although data and address registers behave differently in some ways, they can often be used interchangeably. There is no constraint on which registers can be used to transfer data to external devices, for example, as there is in older 8-bit processors. There are only two important differences between the two types of register:

* address registers connect to both address and data buses
* data registers can handle bytes; address registers can't.

In most cases the two types behave in exactly the same way but important differences will be stressed whenever they crop up.

The status register consists of a system byte and a condition code register. The ccr will concern you from instruction to instruction, as the majority of instructions have some effect on it: but the system byte sets the context of the machine and is comparatively rarely invoked. The ccr contains 5 flags, which we call by their initials: ZNCVX. The system byte contains 2 flags and a 3-bit interrupt mask. The system flags are the S and T flags. We'll get to the meaning of all these later. For now, those of you familiar with other micros will be recognising familiar landmarks, and puzzling about some less familiar features of the landscape. By the end of the book, you'll know whodunnit.

1.2.4 The Memory

Memory is not a part of the processor, but a peripheral device, as peripheral as a printer. But memory is a lot faster than a printer - or any other peripheral - and so we tend to think of it as an integral part of the computer. Since it often lives on the same board, this is no bad thing. The MC68000 can address 16Mb directly, but few sytems are this large, since memory is still fairly expensive.

Memory is a random-access device. This does not mean that memory is entered at random - far from it - but rather that the speed of access is not governed by the address of the data to be accessed. So it's just as fast to access a byte at the top end of memory as one right near the beginning. It's worth bearing in mind, though, that when the speed of access is independent of the actual address, the speed of address calculation imposes a constraint on processor response time. It takes twice as long to calculate a long word address as to calculate a word address. You will see the significance of this observation later on.

1.2.5 The stack pointers

The stack is an area of memory accessed via a pointer called a stack pointer. There are two of these in the MC68000: a supervisor stack pointer for use in supervisor mode, and a user stack pointer for use in user mode. Both of these are located in register a7, so that a7 is one logical register and two physical registers. This may seem an odd arrangement, but you will discover why it makes sense.

1.2.6 The program counter

This tells the MC68000 where to get the next instruction from. This is a memory location, so the program counter has to be at least 24 bits wide. It must also have access to both the data and the address buses.

SECTION 2
Starting with Assembler

This section tells you what machine language is; what an assembler does; what assembler directives are; and what pieces of software are needed to write and run an assembly language program. You will also know about the data types recognised by the MC68000: bits, bcd, bytes, words, long words and pages.

2.1 Assembly language.

2.2 Writing an assembly language program.

2.3 The editor, the assembler, the link editor and the loader.

2.4 Coding conventions.

2.5 Assembler directives.

2.6 Data types.

An Important Note:
A special font is used in this book to distinguish ordinary text from assembler code. An example is:

```
add d0,d1.
```

When necessary, this font is used to distinguish normal text from text that may only appear on the screen.

2.1 Assembly language.

We can take advantage of the facilities of the MC68000 by using a high-level language interpreter or compiler, the features of an operating system, or by writing in the machine's own language. Our applications often dictate the choice we make, assuming the boss is prepared to pay for the software tools we select!

Why use Assembler?

Computer languages can be as simple or as roccoco as you like. BASIC, for example, is simple but somewhat bizarre in some of its manifestations. Forth and 'C' are simple to look at but hard to use. Machine code is incomprehensible to any but real bare metal freaks. Assembler is a fairly moderate compromise in several ways:

* It is direct - you are addressing the machine itself.
* It is spare - the grammar is very simple.
* It is complete - anything the machine does is done ultimately in a transform of assembly language.
* It is unfriendly - you need to work to use it.

A BASIC program is really a succession of calls to functions of varying complexity, so that even a simple statement like 'print a$' triggers off a complex succession of actions inside the processor. In assembly language, you have to write all the instructions for those actions yourself - even if you only have to do it once. So if your life is to be spent writing 'print' programs, stick to BASIC or RPG.

If, on the other hand, you want to write programs for controlling terminals, or for translating BASIC statements, or operating systems, or even print programs which run fast in a restricted space, assembly language is what you need. This is because you can manage the processor, its peripherals and its memory exactly as you wish.

Why is the language called assembly language?

The earliest computers were programmed (in *machine* code) by means of a front panel with a bank of switches on it. A command to load register A with a number, load register B with another, add the two together and put the result into register B might have had to be entered as a sequence of three commands. Each command would consist of at least two parts: the operation code or opcode, and the operand on which the opcode operated. These opcodes would consist of bit patterns; the bit pattern 1101, for example, could have signified 'add', and 1110, 'subtract'. The bit patterns were communicated to the computer by setting switches up for 1, down for 0. As you can imagine, this was laborious, slow and fraught with error. It wasn't long before front panels began to incorporate haxadecimal keypads, so 1101 could be entered as a hex D, and 1110 as a hex E; the hardware itself could convert the hex codes to bit patterns.

A sequence of hex digits is a lot easier to enter than a sequence of switches, but it still doesn't look like anything you or I would be able to recognise in the dark. So the next step is to convert a hex number like 3B to a mnemonic which reminds the programmer of its function: ADD. At this stage, opcodes are represented as mnemonics. A special program stored in the computer, called an assembler, converts these mnemonics to bit patterns using a lookup table, so it has no trouble handling them; and the programmer is reminded of the function of the opcode, so he remembers to supply the correct operands. Life begins to get a whole lot simpler.

2.2 Writing an assembly language program.

A sequence of instructions is a program. If the programmer had to keep track of memory locations, data values and code addresses by hand, he'd take a long, long time to write useful, clean code. The computer can take over a lot of these functions, so making the programmer's job even easier.

2.2.1 Assembler to Machine Code

At this stage the programmer is several stages removed from execution of the instructions. To turn his program into a pattern of binary switches, a lot of things have to happen:

1. The programmer produces a file of instructions in the form of mnemonics. Most variables and addresses are in symbolic form, but can be turned into actual values by simple calculations. This file is called the source file: the code in it is called source code. The source code may contain both machine language instructions and assembler directives, as well as comments.

2. The source code is read by a program called an assembler. The assembler checks that the mnemonics are valid and that operands of the correct type and number are specified for each instruction. If it detects any errors, it will point these out. It also carries out the assembler directives. The comments it ignores. They are of no relevance from now on.

3. The assembler makes a table of all the symbolic values the programmer has used and computes actual values, which it substitutes into the source file. From this point on, directives have no more meaning; and labels and names have been converted to numbers. All expressions have been evaluated.

4. All the mnemonics are converted into hexadecimal opcodes with their operands.

5. The assembler puts the result of its labours into an output file called the object file, which contains object (i.e. machine) code.

6. The source file may contain references to labels in programs outside itself, programs which will be in memory at the same time. In this case the cross-references must be handled by a facility called linking. Most assemblers contain a link editor, but some require linking to be done by a separate link editor.

7. A properly assembled and linked object file has to be loaded into memory at the correct location before it can be executed. The assembler will append loading information to the object file. The file will be loaded by a program called a hexadecimal loader.

An object file can be run on any compatible computer capable of loading it into memory and executing it. The object code is in the machine language of the processor for which the code was assembled. In general, no processor will be able to execute commands written in the machine code of any other processor.

You may think that a Z80A assembler can take MC6809 source code and turn out Z80A object code. However, this is over-optimistic. The two processors have many similiarities but also many differences, so in general there is no guarantee that an operation will be performed by both in the same way. The way flags, registers and addressing modes in particular, are used differs so much between different processors that source code written for one will not carry out the same job in another.

The immediate ancestors of the MC68000, the M6800 and the M6809, can share each other's source code, although the object codes are different and there are some things a 6809 can do and a 6800 can't. However the difference between 8-bit and 16-bit architecture is too large to allow source code compatibility between the 6809 and the 68000. Although Motorola claim that 6809 source code can be assembled for the 68000, it seems much more sensible to rewrite from scratch for the new processor.

2.2.2 Why Write in Assembler ?

Programs written in high-level languages are portable between different machines to a greater or lesser degree. They are also problem-oriented rather than machine-oriented. So why don't we just write in high-level languages, giving assembly language a miss completely?

The answer is that assembler allows you to make full use of all the features of a particular microprocessor, so that you get the best performance out of it in terms of speed and memory usage.

However, size and speed are not usually critical in business applications. Where they *do* count is in real-time control applications, including input-output and operating systems for computers. There are languages specially designed for some such applications, but generally unless you are an expert working more-or-less exclusively in a specialised field you will not even get to hear of them, so when you have applications in which program size and program speed are critical, you will write in assembly language.

This is not to say that there is no use in business for assembly language. There is. It seems that multicoloured graphics with stereo sound are now indispensible in the boardrooms of the land. A balance sheet is no longer enough; the books must now behave like coloratura sopranos. To get these effects in real time (what other kind is there?) you have to go fast, and use memory wisely. You have to write in machine language.

Many high-level languages allow you to include segments of assembler code in a program, which may help you to write the bulk of a large program quickly in the high-level language, using assembler for a critical module, or one which is difficult to implement in the high-level language.

You will also find assembler intellectually satisfying. It allows you to get into the sort of intimate situations with your computer which would be frowned on if the machine were made of flesh and blood rather than MOS. And from the boss's point of view, a piece of commercial software in machine language is a lot easier to protect than the same software in Basic.

2.3 The editor, the assembler, the link editor and the loader.

Before you can produce a machine language program, you will need (in addition to this book, a machine and a comfortable chair) the following:

* a screen editor
* an assembler
* a linker
* a loader

What are all these things for?

It would be tedious to have to get everything right first time, or correct the whole thing, so an editor is an invaluable aid to writing code. There are some editors with tab stops set specially for assembly language writing; if you can get one of these for the 68000, so much the better. But any editor will do.

When the file's written and correct, you'll need an assembler to turn it into a form the machine understands. Suppose you write:

```
abcd (a1),d1
```

This string takes 11 bytes, not counting spaces. The MC68000 would be bound to misunderstand the ASCII literal if it tried to execute it. So, the assembler turns these 11 bytes into a one-word instruction which the MC68000 can execute. The completed file is input to the next stage, the linker. The assembler gives you a listing of your code and its assembled version, usually in this format:

```
memory address   assembled form   unassembled form your comment
hh  hhhh          hhhh  hhhh       verb op          comment
```

The first column is for your information. You can see where the program is to be loaded and where any data will go. The second column will not tell you anything you need to know, but shows you the form in which the instruction is stored in memory. You won't use this column unless you decide to write your own assembler! The third and fourth columns are your original input.

There may be no need for a linker, whose job is to see that external references in one machine-language file are properly resolved in another, to be linked to it for loading. If your file is a complete load module, you won't need a linker - which is also called a link-editor or linkage editor.

The properly-linked file must be loaded into memory. By this time the file is a hexadecimal file, so the loader is often called a hexadecimal loader. The hexadecimal file contains only the assembled instructions and some load information which will be used by the loader to position the file correctly in memory. Its position may always be the same; or the code can be loaded into any available crevice if it's relocatable.

These four tools are often combined into one piece of software (called an assembler) for convenience. It is as well to bear in mind that there are assemblers and assemblers. Some assemblers may not allow macro expansion. Some may be fussy about symbols. Some are one-pass assemblers, which do everything on one pass through your file. Some are two-pass assemblers, which spend the first pass collecting tokens for a symbol table. The facilities assemblers offer will differ from one to the other. To make learning as easy as possible, try to restrict your use of different assemblers, and when this is impossible, try to find a common subset of each.

2.3.1 Source code

The source file which you produce for your assembler will contain some of the following:

* source code mnemonics
* assembler directives
* labels and names
* comments
* expressions

The source code mnemonics are defined for you by Motorola. There are 72 of them, which doesn't sound like much. However, most can be used with byte, word or double-word operands and a large selection of 11 addressing modes. This results in more than 2000 distinct commands. (If this is still not enough for you, you may like to try writing microcode for the undefined opcodes.)

The assembler directives are defined by the provider of the assembler and differ, as we have said, from one to another - although there is a fairly standard subset.

Comments, labels and names are for you to provide - within the constraints imposed by your system, particularly on names and labels. The rules you should follow are:

* Make names and labels meaningful:
    - 'testp1' rather than 'floog1'
    - 'daynum' rather than 'ndy' (for number of day in year)
* Avoid confusion:
    - 'testio' and 'test10'
    - 'hoho' and 'hohoho' (banned under rule 1 anyway)
* Don't use reserved words
* Comment obscure points, not everything
* A comment is as important as its code, not less so
* Start a name or a label with a letter, not a number

The assembler has its own rules about names and labels. You are usually restricted to a maximum of 6 or 8 characters which may be alpha or numeric, with a letter to start. Some assemblers ignore trailing characters, others simply blow up. Some assemblers can distinguish between upper and lower case, some cannot. Usually, a label must start in the first column to be recognised as such. Some assemblers recognise special characters in labels and names; most commonly, the underscore. Try to avoid them, because the next time you're using a different assembler, it'll have different preferences.

Assembly language is very simple indeed. There are only two parts of speech, the *verb* and the *noun*. The forms of sentence allowed are:

* v
* v n
* v n n

A sentence conforming to one of these patterns is called an instruction, the mood of the machine verb being imperative only!

A verb (alias opcode, mnemonic) is one of the 72 in the instruction set. A noun must be:

* a register
* a number
  - binary
  - octal
  - decimal
  - hexadecimal
* an ASCII character
* a name
* a label
* an expression

Why such a simple language should bring terror to the hearts of grown programmers is a mystery. Possibly there are still too many race memories of nights spent huddled in the cave, the wind howling and the sabre-tooth growling outside, while instructions were coded laboriously in switches on a front panel (what's that, Daddy?).

Those 72 verbs fall naturally into groups. Although some people may divide them into more- and less-frequently used, this can become a vicious circle: you learn them, use them and ignore the others. It's more instructive to look at the verbs in functional groups. There is a group of verbs for moving data, a group for doing mathematics, a group of logical operators and several others. Sometimes I represent a group by a verb which is not part of the instruction set but characterizes the whole group. This I call a *pseud*. This may be an unnecessary elaboration, but it saves a lot of repetition.

Assembler *directives* are not instructions to the processor, but instructions to the assembler. They don't relate to the problem you are solving, but to the program you have written to solve the problem. They vary between assemblers although there are some standard directives. In general, the more versatile an assembler, the greater the range of directives it offers.

Labels are names for sections of the program. They save you the trouble of remembering actual values. The assembler keeps a table of labels and their values, substituting a value into the program whenever you use a label.

23

Comments are there to help you understand what your program is doing. You may begrudge the time spent writing them, but there is nothing more frustrating than writing very clever code and being quite unable to understand it the next day, unless it's writing deceptively simple code which you alter without understanding its full significance. The altered code may turn you into a lifelong opiate addict. If it's so easy for you to forget the meaning of your code, think how much easier it would be for a total stranger whose only connection with you is a ream of unintelligible gunk. Such people have been driven to resort to voodoo to get their revenge.

Arithmetic and logical operators are used by the assembler at assembly time to evaluate expressions in your code. The result of this evaluation goes into your program, not the expression itself. To illustrate this, consider an expression in an instruction like this:

```
move #a+b*c, (a0)
```

When the program is assembled, the assembler will find values for a, b and c, evaluate the expression and get a result. Let's assume this is 15. It will take your instruction to mean:

```
move #15, (a0)
```

If you use an expression in an effort to avoid a little work, all you do is end up making your program look a little murkier than it should. If, on the other hand, the expression illustrates the derivation of the operand, its use is a form of selfdocumentation and therefore laudable. Look at this example:

```
pea #filestrt(a5,d6)
```

Here we have calculated the address of the start of a field in a record and put it into the operand field. filestrt is a name which will have been defined earlier using an assembler directive:

```
filestrt EQU $4000+4*256+80
```

Bear in mind that the expression will only be evaluated once, at assembly time, yielding a result which will be fixed for all subsequent runs of the assembled code.

Although there are several MC68000 assemblers on the market, all slightly different from each other, they all follow the same broad conventions. Whenever you encounter an assembler with which you are unfamiliar, read the manual rather than make assumptions. Any boss who knows the business will pay you for the time it takes.

24

2.4 Coding conventions.

The standard Motorola assembler uses these conventions:

* There is one instruction per line.
* There must be at least one space before the verb.
* There must be at least one space after the verb.
* Two operands are separated only by a comma - no spaces.
* A comment must be preceded by at least one space.
* A line beginning with an asterisk is a comment.
* Only the first 8 characters of labels are meaningful.
* The first character of a label is uppercase alpha or a period.
* Subsequent characters may be
    - uppercase alpha
    - a digit
    - one of the four special characters . # _ $
* Labels start in the first column and end in a space OR
* Labels start anywhere and end in a colon.
* The base of a number must be specified to the assembler:
    - a leadingt $ signifies hexadecimal
    - a leading Q signifies octal
    - a leading % signifies binary
    - ASCII literals are enclosed in single quotes
    - the default is decimal

Don't try to use mnemonics or assembler directives as labels. It may work but it's not smart to push your assembler to its limits.

It is smart to use the base that makes the most sense in a particular case. It's dumb to write $48, $45, $4C, $4C, $4F instead of 'HELLO'. On the other hand, a bit pattern is best specified in binary, because then you can actually see the thing. There doesn't seem to me to be much virtue in being able to visualize the bit pattern for $F6 and writing that instead of %11110110, and if there is, it just makes life hard for the less virtuous who end up as maintenance programmers.

As we've seen, arithmetic expressions are allowed in an operand field. The operators allowed in expressions are, in order of precedence:

›› and ‹‹ for shift left and shift right
$ for AND, ! for OR
the arithmetic operators + - * /

The portion of an expression in brackets () is evaluated first, followed by the operators in order of precedence. Those with the same rank are evaluated from left to right.

You may need to use an expression in an address field - as we did in our example. When you do so, make sure that the resultant address is within permissible limits. If the result is an address in the middle of your operating system, you could make a lot of enemies.

2.5 Assembler directives.

Directives are instructions to the assembler to do particular things during assembly without generating any object code corresponding with the directive. The simplest directive is END. This means what it says: here endeth this program, so you can stop assembling now. This is not the same as the verb stop.

Other directives fall naturally into groups. There is a group which reserves memory, with or without initializing it:

```
RESERVE
DATA
DS
DC
DCB
```

Each of these is used on a line with a name at the beginning and some more information after it:

```
IOBUFFER RESERVE 256
PROMPT DATA "Please key in your access code:'
```

DS means "Define storage":

```
CUSNAM: DS.W 30
```

This reserves 30 words of space and identifies it with the label CUSNAM, so it works much the same as RESERVE. It does not place anything in these 30 words, unlike DATA, which is used to put a definite value into a labelled location.

DC means 'define constant':

```
FACTOR: DC.L $0010FFFF
```

This sets aside space for a constant called FACTOR and initializes that space to the value on the right.

DCB means 'define constant block':

```
BUFF: DCB.B 30, ' '
```

This defines a block of 30 spaces.

DS, DC and DCB are all used with a suffix to indicate whether a word, byte or long word is intended. There is no default: you must specify the data size. The MC68000 has a rule that all instructions begin on a word boundary, so if you reserve an odd number of bytes of memory, the assembler pads out the location with an extra byte to comply with this rule. If in doubt, the EVN directive can be used to enforce this.

There are two directives which assign values to names but these values are then used at assembly time, rather than being evaluated for use at execution time. These are EQU and SET.

```
SIX EQU 6
```

means 'set the value of the name SIX to 6'. This value will be retained throughout the assembly of the program.

```
SIX SET 6
```

has the same meaning, but it allows a little more flexibility in that you are free later in the assembly to say

```
SIX SET 7
```

and the label SIX will now take on its new value.

ORG and SECTION are used to show where blocks of code, data or memory areas are to begin. SECTION is used with a linkage editor to create relocatable code. There may be several origins in one program, for data, program, subroutines and so on. Each is specified by means of the ORG directive:

```
PROGRAM EQU $4000
ORG PROGRAM
```

The effect of this is to say:

* the name PROGRAM has the value $4000
* set the origin to PROGRAM i.e. to $4000

We could just as well write:

```
ORG $4000
```

All this directive does is set the assembler's location counter - which tells it where in memory it is inserting code or data - to a given value. So here we are putting in program at $4000. Later, after putting in a couple of kilobytes, we may want to insert data at another fixed location, so we could then say:

```
ORG $8000
```

Now the location counter is set to $8000 and anything we put in from now on begins there. There is nothing to stop us using a lower value than that of the current location counter; it's up to us to make sure that it makes sense.

In some assemblers there are directives like MACRO or INCLUDE which include code from a library file or expand a section of code a certain number of times. You may find that a section of code repeats often in your program. Give this section a name, and use the name instead of the code at subsequent locations. The assembler will replace all occurrences of the name by the code going under that name:

```
MACRO MAC
 --    --
 --    --
 --    --
 --    --
ENDM
```

Now whenever you include a line saying simply

```
MAC
```

the lines between MACRO MAC and ENDM will appear at this place in the listing.

This is not the same as a subroutine: there is only one copy of a subroutine in the object code, but there is a copy of the macro for every occurrence of the name.

INCLUDE in some assemblers will include a block of code from a library file:

```
INCLUDE LIBFIL
```

will look for LIBFIL and read it into the source code at this point. You may be able to specify a section of the file:

```
INCLUDE LIBFIL,SEC2
```

Most assemblers have facilities for conditional assembly, in which the assembler makes tests and, depending on the result, includes or excludes blocks of source code from the object file.

```
IF SWITCH1


  -- -- --
  -- -- --
  -- -- --
  -- -- --
ENDIF
```

If at assembly time SWITCH1 is true, the code between the IF and the ENDIF will be included in the assembly. This feature is especially useful for creating run-time packages including only those features of a system which are actually used by an application.

A great deal of thought has gone into writing assemblers and although a lot of their facilities may seem arcane when first encountered, a closer study will reveal their benefits. Once again, there is no substitute whatsoever for a more-than-cursory perusal of the manual.

2.6 Data types.

The MC68000 can handle various combinations of bits:

Bit
Byte
BCD
Word
Long word
Page

A bit can be in one of two states represented by 0 or 1 which is why some people say the word is from binary digit. (I prefer to think that this is folk etymology and that computer people sensibly used the smallest intelligible word for the smallest unit of data.)

Eight bits form a byte. There are 256 possible combinations of 8 bits on or off, so there are 256 different 8-bit bytes.

Two bytes together form a word, two words a long word. There are 65,536 different 16-bit words and 4 x 1024 x 1024 x 1024 different 32-bit long words.

Four bits in a byte can exist in 16 different states. Humans count in 10s - at any rate in most cases. Three bits will only give us 8 combinations. So at the cost of a little waste, the MC68000 is set up to use four bits to represent a single decimal digit. This is referred to as binary-coded decimal representation.

Binary arithmetic may be performed on numbers in one of two ways:

* by regarding the numbers as signed
* by regarding the numbers as unsigned

A single byte may represent unsigned numbers from 0 to 255: 00 is zero, FF is 255. If this byte is signed, bit 7 is regarded as a sign bit. If bit 7 is 0, the sign is +; if bit 7 is 1, the sign is −. This then means that $FF is regarded as −1, and $80 as −128. The highest positive value the byte can hold is $7F, which is 127. So the range of signed numbers in a byte is −128 to +127, which is −2^7 to 2^7−1.

This can be generalised:

n bits can hold 2^n different numbers.
If these numbers are unsigned, they range from 0 to 2^n-1.
If these numbers are signed, they range from -2^{n-1} to $2^{n-1}-1$.

A signed, negative byte has bit 7 = 1.
A signed, negative word has bit 15 = 1.
A signed, negative long word has bit 31 = 1.

You will find that there are good reasons for addressing memory in 64kb chunks. Each such chunk is called a page. Of particular interest to us are the bottom and top pages of memory. There are 256 64kb pages in the memory space of the MC68000: and 64k pages in the 68020.

Memory mapping

It is worth considering that not all the memory of an MC68000 is actually memory. Some of it may be assigned to devices. Consider as an example a monitor screen with 512 pixels across and 256 down. This is a fairly high-resolution screen. Instead of referring to the dots on the screen via some port, the processor may treat them exactly as if they were memory. Such a screen contains 128k bit positions which could be stored in 16kb of memory. If the external screen is itself treated as a memory device, each bit of the screen could be addressed by the processor by means of a memory address. Such an arrangement is called memory mapping.

SECTION 3
Instructions and Modes

At last we come to the crunch: the MC68000 machine language instruction set. Here we tabulate the instructions before going on to descibe the address modes. Without understanding how the machine locates data and programs, you would find it difficult or impossible to write sensible instructions. This section tells you how the machine finds its way around memory as it carries out your instructions.

When you've finished this section, you will have encountered the 72 instructions in the instruction set and the 11 address modes available. You will also have been introduced to the concept of the address mode group.

3.1 The instruction set.

3.2 Address modes.

3.1 The instruction set.

Fig. 3.1 is a table of all the verbs in MC68000 machine language. These are repeated in the Appendix, which also contains information on address mode groups and ccr effects. Look up in the Appendix anything which puzzles you.

add	sub	abcd	sbcd	muls	divs
addi	subi	addx	subx	mulu	divu
addq	subq	nbcd	negx		
adda	suba				
neg	not			bchg	bset
		bra	bsr	bclr	btst
		jmp	jsr		
move				tas	tst
movea		bcc	dbcc	cmp	chk
movem		scc		cmpa	
movep				cmpm	
moveq					
swap		link	unlk	and	or eor
exg		pea	lea	andi	ori eori
ext					
		trap	trapv	asl	asr
rte				lsl	lsr
rtr		nop	illegal	rol	ror
rts		reset	stop	roxl	roxr

Fig.3.1 The MC68000 Instruction Set (Verbs are grouped by function)

If we study the verbs in these groups we will be able to learn about a number of related verbs at once, as well as understanding more easily some otherwise puzzling aspects of address modes and the condition codes.

35

3.2 Address modes.

All a microprocessor or any other kind of computer can do is shove data around. The way in which it does this makes it appear intelligent, which should give you pause for thought about your own activities. The power of the MC68000 instruction set lies in the number of different ways in which the processor can find the data it needs: *the addressing modes*.

There are 11 addressing modes available, all of which are used to address either registers or memory. Beginners find the names confusing, so I intend to explain the modes and add the names as an afterthought. I think it is true to say that there are few programmers who can rattle off the names of all the address modes they use; but there are virtually no programmers who can't use them all.

The MC68000 usually has a 24-bit address bus. A 6809 or a Z80A has a 16-bit address bus. Sixteen bits represent 216 different numbers, which is 64*1024 or 64k or 65586. So a 16-bit address bus can have 64k different addresses on it, which is why an 8-bit computer can address 64k of memory directly. Of course, some pretty respectable 8-bit computers, like the SWTPC S/09 which runs on a Motorola M6809, can address a lot more than 64k, but they do it by means of special memory management techniques, not by directly addressing this memory.

A 32-bit address bus can address 2^{32} different locations directly. This is $(64k)^2$ or 4 gigabytes of memory - enough to run a small government department - that is until Parkinson's Law begins to operate. The MC68000 only uses 24 of these 32 bits, making it capable of addressing 16 megabytes directly. This is good news for those systems programmers who have to fit a full graphics screen, a good DOS and a high-level interpreter into a micro and still leave room for a spreadsheet and a DBMS in user memory, allowing half a dozen users to use the whole caboodle at once.

Most computers using the MC68000 have a minimum of 128k of memory. Only 15 years ago a lot of big business was running on mainframes with only 64k, so 128k is adequate for many applications. In a multiuser, multitasking environment, more memory is often needed and so a UNIX-based system would tend to have a minimum of 256k, largely because it becomes rather slow when it has less than this and more than about four users.

36

The addressing modes are simply ways of finding your way around all this memory. It would obviously be a little difficult to remember just where you put everything in a memory this large - I find it hard to find my way around a tiny carbon memory - but the addressing modes available lighten the burden considerably.

Immediate addressing

One way of locating the data you want is to include it in the instruction:

```
add #9099,d1
    :add the value 9099 to register d1
```

Here the # sign signifies that the value which follows is the actual value of the required data. Because the data follows immediately after the verb, this form of addressing is called immediate addressing. An intermediate hexadecimal operand needs an additional prefix:

```
add #$9099,d1
    :add hexadecimal 9099 to register d1
```

It is a little unusual for a value in a program to be exactly the same run after run after run. The exceptions are certain physical or mathematical constants, but even values like π may sometimes be put into a table rather than directly into program memory. You may write a program to calculate VAT and include a line specifying the VAT rate:

```
move.b #15,d1
    :move the value 15 to register d1
```

If the boss likes your program (because it works - there's precious little other cause for liking a program), it may be burned into rom and thousands sold. One day the Chancellor, finding a small war and a smaller surplus on his hands, raises VAT to 22%. All you've got to do now is get those thousands of roms back and replace them with chips containing the assembled line:

```
move.b #22,d1
```

Direct addressing

Life would have been much simpler had you written:

```
move $2000,d1
```

You could have included some means such as read from a file or keyboard for getting the value 15 (pre-war) or 22 (after the bomb) into memory location $2000. This mode of addressing is called direct, because the address is a direct address: but Motorola call it absolute short addressing. It's called short because only one word of address data is included, and absolute because this is absolutely the address you need.

You know that addresses consist of 24 bits, so what does the machine do about the high-order byte of the address? If you think it pads it with 0s, you're absolutely half-right: it extends the sign. If the sign is 0, the high-order byte it uses is all 0s. If the sign is negative, the high-order byte is all 1s, so this is what happens:

* Any address nnnn less than 8000 becomes 00nnnn
* Any address nnnn greater than 7FFF becomes FFnnnn

The beauty of this is that it allows you to address the bottom 64k of memory in any system directly, using absolute short addressing and positive addresses. But this is not all, because if you use negative addresses - with bit 15 of the address word set to 1 - you address the top 64k of memory, wherever that may be located. This gives a convenient way of accessing more memory than most 8-bit computers have on board.

Of course, the existence of short addressing implies the existence of long addressing, and sure enough this exists too. In this mode, the programmer supplies 3 bytes which can specify an address anywhere in the memory that the MC68000 can access:

```
move $60FF07,d1
```

Although the low word of the address given here is $FF07, the memory page - given by the top byte - is 60. Absolute long addressing allows us to address all 256 64k pages of memory. Note that the implied operand length is one word, but the address given is long. There is no conflict here. Look at these three instructions:

```
move.b $60FF07,d1
move $60FF07,d1
move.l $60FF07,d1
```

In the first case, the byte at the given address is involved; in the second case, 2 bytes at that address are moved; in the third case, 4 bytes are moved. The length is the length of the actual operand, not of its address.

These two instructions look similar, but they are very different:

```
add $0090,d0
add #$0090,d0
```

In the first case, the operator is in data memory; in the second case, it is in program memory. This distinction is worth knowing about because it aids understanding of the modes available for different instructions.

In the first case the processor puts $000090 on the address bus and adds what comes off the data bus to d0. The second instruction means "Add the value $0090 to register d0". Here the value is not an address, but actual data, so this is what goes onto the data bus and into d0. Here there is room for error, and you should make sure that you appreciate the difference between the two modes.

Think what happens if you do this in a banking program:

```
sub #$0090,d1 ;$0090 contains withdrawal
            ; d1 is balance after withdrawal
```

Everyone withdraws hexadecimal 90 (i.e. decimal £144), no matter what they withdraw, and another computer gets badmouthed unfairly, or blamed for human crimes.

Register direct

So far one operand has been somewhere in memory and the other in a data register. We sometimes use two registers:

```
add d0,d1
```

This adds the low word in d0 to the low word in d1. This form of addressing is called register direct, for fairly obvious reasons, and is simple enough to understand. In the early days of computers it was about the only address mode available: everything had to be in registers. There are still some visible-record computers, on active service, using this mode and this mode only.

39

Address register indirect

The register may contain, not the data itself but the address of the data:

rol (a6)

Here there is an item of data somewhere in memory. Its precise address is not known - or rather not shown - but we know that this address is held in a6. So we say in effect:

- get an address from a6
- get the data at this address
- rotate this data 1 bit left
- restore the data to its resting place.

If we didn't have this address register indirect address mode, we'd have a lot more coding to do. (Because I like abbreviations I call address register indirect *ari*. You will do the same for the duration of this book.)

It is maybe a little redundant to talk of address register indirect, because there is no data register indirect mode, addresses being held naturally enough in address registers. Indeed the MC68000 does not allow memory indirect addressing either, so the only form of indirect addressing available for the machine is address register indirect. We could therefore call this simple indirect addressing, but the abbreviation for this is rather too cryptic, even for my liking.

We may be dealing with a data structure, so that we are interested in successive bytes in memory. We may wish to move a record from an input buffer to an output buffer, for example. This is easy with an incrementing version of the *ari* mode:

move (a5)+,(a6)+

This amounts to saying:

Move data whose address is in a5 to the address in a6
Increment the two address registers.

The availability of this *ari* mode with postincrement, abbreviated to ari+ saves us the bother of incrementing the registers by hand after each operation.

ari+ has a sibling, *-ari*:

```
abcd -(a5),-(a6)
```

This is *ari* with predecrement and is equivalent to saying:

- decrement a5
- decrement a6
- decimal add the two bytes pointed to by these registers

-ari and *ari*+ are used for handling the stack. Instead of having two special verbs push and pull for this purpose, the MC68000 uses its handyman move, with these two modes:

```
move d6,-(a7)
```

This puts the contents of register d6 on top of the stack.

```
move (a7)+,d6
```

This pulls the word at the top of the stack off and puts it into d6. This glimpse of stack handling has illustrated some of the salient points about the MC68000's stack:

* it grows downwards like a stalactite, so the top occupies the lowest address
* a7 is the stack pointer
* any address register can use *ari*+ and *-ari*, so any address register can be used as a stack pointer.

Notice that I talk of incrementing, but carefully avoid mentioning the size of the increment. This is simply because the machine takes care of the size automatically, incrementing by 1, 2 or 4, depending on the size of the operand. Remember that the size of the operand is postfixed to the verb, with these results:

```
move.b -(a7),d6    moves a byte & decrements a7 by 1
move.w -(a7),d6    moves 2 bytes & decrements a7 by 2
move -(a7),d6      is the same - the default length is word
move.l -(a7),d6    moves 4 bytes & increments a7 by 4
```

ari, -ari and *ari*+ are extremely versatile address modes and you'll find that you come to rely very heavily on them. But there are, of course, other, simpler address modes and more complicated ones too.

Program Counter Relative

The program counter may be used to calculate addresses, and this is especially useful in multiuser systems where your code may be loaded anywhere in memory yet be expected to operate successfully all the time. Such code is called relocatable or position independent.

```
move *+$256,d7
```

"Move the data $256 bytes from the start of the current instruction to register d7". This is *program counter relative addressing*.

Index and Offset Modes

These address modes are sufficient for a large part of your work, but there comes a time when it is handy to include displacements and indexes (don't tell me there's another plural!) to make the address modes more versatile. So we have four additional address modes:

* ari with index - *arix*
* ari with offset - *ario*
* ari with index and offset - *arixo*
* pcr with index - *pcrx*

Let's look at why we have them.

Data structures seldom have only one dimension and in fact a disk file, for example, often has three:

* File start address
* Record start address
* Field start address

Handling data structures is made easier by the use of two extensions to ari. Look at the problem of accessing the nth record in a file of fixed-length records. We can calculate the distance from the start of the file, knowing n and the record length. If the start of the file is in an address register and the offset from the start in a data register, we can write an instruction like this:

```
move (a5,d5),d4
```

"Move the word at a5+d5 to d4". This is ari with index or *arix*, the index register being d5. Any register may be used as an index register.

To get the nth word within the record, we may add a constant offset:

```
move $20(a5,d5),d4
```

This will get the word at position 32 within the record. We call this address mode arix with offset - *arixo*. We also have ario - that is ari with offset but no index. (The literature talks indifferently of offset and displacement.)

Position independent code will work wherever it happens to be located in memory. When the code is loaded, the operating system under which it is running will know the initial value of the program counter. If all subsequent address references are given relative to the program counter the code is position independent.

pcr addressing is itself useful enough but it is enhanced by the inclusion of an index register:

```
pea $20(pc,d1)
```

This means:

add $20 to the current value of the pc and d1
put the resulting address on the stack

A little thought will convince you that the result is hardly different from arixo.

Inherent (implied) addressing

There are some verbs which don't need any help from you, as they know where to find their data or don't need any data at all.

reset, which sends a strobe to all external devices and resets them, is one which needs no data at all. Nor does nop. Motorola says these use inherent addressing. So be it.

rts, rte and rtr know that the data they want are on the stack, so you don't have to tell them anything else. They use the stack pointer and the program counter, and rte and rtx use status register and condition code register respectively. This is also referred to as inherent addressing. More apt is the term implied addressing.

Which Address Mode?

Once you are familiar with all the address modes available you still have the problem of knowing which to use where. The address modes fall into 6 different groups. Each verb characteristically uses all the modes in one of these groups. Initially you may see no rhyme or reason for the groups, but when you've been using machine language for a while, you will suddenly perceive the logic behind them, and reasons for the occasional exceptions.

We have two tables in the Appendices (Section 11). One (Appendix 11.3) shows the address mode goups. The other shows which verbs use those groups. These tables are for reference, not to be learned by rote. The Appendix refers to these tables and if you get occasional odd results, you should refer to them too.

Learn to use the address modes flexibly. You'll be surprised how much easier it is to write good code when you have mastered them all and know when to use which, and how.

SECTION 4
Stacks, Registers and Modes

This section tells you why we use a stack and how; it describes the status register, emphasizing particularly the role of the condition code register. You will learn the difference between supervisor and user modes, and about the interrupt mask.

4.1 Stack handling.

4.2 The status register.

4.3 The condition code register

4.4 Processor modes.

4.1 Stack handling.

4.1.1 Labile memory - the stack

Humans need a bit of scrap paper for even the most basic tasks, just to keep track of what they're doing. Picture Bob Scratchit poring over large open ledgers, with a scap of paper to hand for the intermediate figuring which musn't go into the books and which Ebenezer Scrooge doesn't want to see in the margins either. Computers have the same requirements. They must use some kind of scratchpad memory to keep track of intermediate numbers which they are at liberty to forget as soon as these have served their purpose. The problem is that they may find themselves using an area of memory someone else wants; or that someone else may come along and scribble all over the area of memory they're using, with dire results.

Computers get around this problem by using a stack as a temporary storage area. This is an area of memory whose starting location is known to the programmer. From that point on, it's under processor control. An item is put onto the stack. The processor knows it has used, say, 4 bytes; so it tells itself that the next available location on the stack is 4 bytes from the start in one or other direction. When something has to be retrieved, the processor takes whatever is on the top of the stack off and presents it to the program. It knows now that the stack is a little shorter, and reminds itself of that fact. From this it is obvious that the programmer never knows exactly where an item is located on the stack; nor is there any need to know. It should also be obvious that if the stack is left to proliferate, it can grow to take up all of memory, like some kind of silicon coral reef. The processor normally makes no check to see that the stack is not writing all over program memory.

Using the Stack

The processor keeps track of the stack by means of a stack pointer, which is an address register containing the address of the last byte on the stack. Whenever anything is added to the stack, the stack pointer is decremented (because it grows downward) and whenever anything is pulled from the stack, the stack pointer is incremented. So at any time, the programmer knows where to find the address of some item, but doesn't know where the item itself lives.

The stack pointer is register a7. Remember that this register has two parts, a supervisor and a user portion. If you write to a7 in supervisor mode, change mode and read from a7, you will not read what you

47

have just written. We can represent the two registers as sa7 - the supervisor portion - and ua7.

At start-up time sa7 is initialized to some value set by the systems programmer - which may be you, when you're a competent assembler programmer. This value is stored in the lowest word of available memory, which would be shown in an interrupt vector table. ua7 is initialized by the supervisor. From this point on, the stack is used as temporary storage, most frequently in connection with subroutines and the gsr verbs.

A *gsr* is an instruction to go away, do something and come back to the next instruction when that's completed. There are two *gsr* opcodes available: jsr and bsr.

jsr is a long jump to an address anywhere in the 16 megabytes of memory a MC68000 can address:

```
jsr address
:    jump to the subroutine at the absolute address
```

This is an absolute jump, because address is the actual destination, no matter what the current value of the program counter when jsr is executed. The jump may be short – within 64k bytes, or long – to anywhere at all in the MC68000's memory space.

bsr is a relative branch to a subroutine somewhere in the 64k memory page the bsr itself lives in:

```
bsr offset
: branch to the address given by (pc + offset)
```

offset may be a byte or a word, and gives access either to the 256 bytes around the program counter, or the whole page around it. It is a relative jump because the destination is dependent on the value of the program counter at the time the instruction is carried out, so you can't always tell from reading the code where the branch will end up; you have to know where the program is loaded, too.

You can see therefore that jsr takes longer to execute than bsr, and destroys the position independence of the subroutine. This doesn't mean that jsr has no place in good programming, because programs often access subroutines in fixed locations elsewhere - in the operating system, for example.

4.1.2 Interrupts

There are other ways of jumping to a subroutine. An interrupt or an exception will cause a transfer of control in exactly the same way as a jsr, but with some additional processing. The status register must be saved, for example; this is saved on the stack. A subroutine is any piece of code ending in an *rtx*. This pragmatic definition saves a lot of philosophical agonizing. There are three types of *rtx*:

* rts: the undoer of gsr
* rti: return from interrupt
* rte: return from exception

Each of these finds its way back to the calling routine via the stack. Let's see how this works:

```
jsr label means move pc,-(a7)
              move label,pc
bsr label means move pc,-(a7)
              add label,pc
```

Now the program counter contains the address of the subroutine and the stack holds the address of the byte after the gsr. The stack pointer points to the last byte pushed onto the stack, because the processor works out the size of the step from the word length of the operand: 1 for a byte, 2 for a word, 4 for a long word. The last filled location on the stack is called the top of the stack, even though the stack grows downward with each predecrement.

The processor goes through the subroutine until it comes to an rtx.

This is what happens now:

```
rtx means move (a7)+,pc
```

The program counter gets the address of the byte following the gsr from the stack, puts this address into the program counter and fetches the next instruction from this location. Here are at least two opportunities for error. Human nature being what it is, they are opportunities that no-one passes up, so you should be fully aware of their dangers:

49

* If the value at the top of the stack is not the proper return address, you're in trouble.
* If the address pointed to contains data instead of a valid opcode, you're in more trouble.

To avoid problems of the first kind, keep the stack tidy. Remember that it's a first-in, first-out storage area, so unstack in the reverse order from stacking. To avoid the second kind of problem, don't write programs which mix data and code at any time, and in particular, look out for lines like:

```
jsr label1
dc.b variable
```

When the processor comes back to the byte after the jsr, it'll load variable into the instruction register, with totally unpredictable consequences.

As you can see, we use postincrement to pull from the stack, predecrement to push to it. Now perhaps you appreciate the utility of these addressing modes. If you are familiar with other assemblers, you will have noted that there are no push and pop instructions, their place being taken by move; and that the stack pointer points to the item on top of the stack and not to the next location, as it would in the 6809, for example.

4.1.3 Reentrant code

If all the stack does is keep track of return addresses, stack handling should present few problems: but the stack has another, equally important purpose. It enables you to write reentrant code. What do we mean by reentrant? Imagine a subroutine subrx, which produces a 32-bit word as output.

> proga calls subrx, which begins to work out the result.
> Along comes progb, with a higher priority than proga.
> progb interrupts subrx, and gets it to do a new calculation.

If subrx keeps its results in a fixed area of memory, progb's results will overwrite those of proga. progb will get what it asked for, but proga gets chop suey. Obviously, subrx is no use if it gets interrupted.

The stack provides one solution: subrx starts by pushing all the registers it uses onto the stack, thus saving their current values. Remember that a subroutine has no way of knowing whether it is interrupting or is being interrupted or not. Next, the results are calculated. Usually, they reside in registers. They must be saved - say, on the stack.

When the subroutine is finished, it retrieves the saved registers from the stack before pulling its return address. The subroutine which has been interrupted is now reentrant: because the registers were saved and restored, the interrupted subroutine comes back to find things exactly as it left them. This type of code allows you to write modular systems which can do multitasking or accommodate several users at once. This is not the whole story of reentrant code, which needs a book of its own, but it underlines the principles.

The stack is used by exceptions as well as in processing gsr verbs. Various registers and status information, as well as the program counter, are pushed onto the stack at the start of exception processing and restored when an rte is executed. This is something to bear in mind if ever you write a language compiler: error processing can make you lose your place in the stack.

We've been using the pseud *rtx* to represent both rts and rtr. The latter is 'return and restore' and works like this:

```
rtr means move (a7)+,sr
            move (a7)+,pc
```

The rtr pulls the first word from the stack and uses it to restore the condition code portion of the status register (*sr*). It does not attempt to restore the high byte of the sr because that's a supervisor function; but it does pull a word, not a byte, from the stack. The effect of this is to restore the values of the flags to their state before the subroutine was entered - particularly useful in arithmetic operations.

There is a catch here, of course: how was the *sr* put onto the stack? The answer is that you have to put it there yourself - and you should do that immediately you enter the subroutine:

```
subrx
      move sr,-(a7)
      ....
      ....
      rtr
```

Obviously, you want to be doubly sure that you've kept the stack tidy so that you restore actual condition codes and not some kind of hash.

The MC68000 allows you to use any address register as a stack pointer. It's therefore useful to use some register other than a7 when writing and debugging. Do this by choosing a register you're not using for anything else and initializing it:

```
subrx
      move #$07ff,a0
```

Now a0 has been initialized as your stack pointer and you can use it exactly as you use a7. When you've debugged the routine and the stack is tidy, use an editor to replace all occurrences of a0 in the routine by a7.

Needless to say, you need the memory map when initializing stack pointers. It will tell you where you can't put a stack, and you will update it to remind yourself where the stack has actually gone. This may sound trivial, but failure to attend to it leads to needless wear and tear on programmer's grey matter. Part of the documentation of your routine is an explicit statement of what stacking, if any, takes place in it.

4.1.5 Linking

There is another way of handling the needs of a particular subroutine for stack space. This is by means of the link instruction:

```
subrx
      link An #block  means move an,-(a7)
                            move a7,an
                            addi #block,a7
```

What's happening here?
    * The programmer specifies an address register *an*
    * The programmer specifies a block *block*
    * The contents of *an* are saved on the stack
    * *a7*'s contents are duplicated in *an*
    * *block* is added to *a7*
    * Note that *block* is a negative value

The net effect is that a block of memory in the stack has been saved for the exclusive use of this subroutine. This block can be as large as you like. All your local variables will go into it, so that they can live in safety during the subroutine but can evaporate outside it. Of course, it makes sense to free the block as soon as you have finished with it:

```
unlk An  means move an,a7
             move (a7)+an
             subi #block,a7
```

* *an* is duplicated in *a7*, leaving *a7* as it was before link
* the old value of *an* is retrieved from the stack
* the block of memory is free

Everything has been restored to the position at the start of the subroutine.

unlk should be the last instruction in a subroutine with link; and link should be the first instruction in the subroutine after any move sr.

Note that link and unlk both involve moving a7. If you tried to write the sequence of instructions represented by link or unlk when in user mode, you'd get a privilege violation because only in supervisor mode can you move a7. However, you can use link/unlk in either mode. Mode switching gives you another opportunity for error: if you switch to user mode in a subroutine, the next time you read a7, you read ua7. But you've actually written sa7; so you don't get back your return address, but whatever happens to be on top of ua7.

The stacking facilities of the MC68000 make it easy to write structured, modular code which is easy to understand and modify. The UNIX operating system makes extensive use of these facilities. The FORTH language, too, uses the stack almost to the exclusion of anything else. This makes FORTH popular in Dnalop, to which Reverse Polish Notation tends to confine it.

4.2 The status register.

The status register (*sr*) to which we have referred occasionally is a sort of scratchpad area that keeps the processor informed of what has happened and the environment in which it has happened. It consists of two parts, the supervisor byte and the condition code register or *ccr*.

The supervisor byte sets the tone of the proceedings by ensuring that allowable interrupts are enabled, unwanted interrupts are disabled and the right people are allowed to use the machine. Bit 7 is the supervisor bit. When this bit is set the processor is in supervisor mode; when it is clear, the processor is in user mode. This is explained further on.

Bit 5 is the trace bit. When this is set, after every instruction the processor takes a detour to reveal to the user the status of the machine. Typically, the registers, the program counter and the status register itself are printed out when a trace is executed.

Bits 2, 1 and 0 form the interrupt mask. All interrupts of higher priority than the mask are allowed; those of the lower priority are disabled. Those of the same priority as the mask are disabled, except for level 7.

The supervisor byte is seldom relevant to what you are doing. You will be much more interested in the low byte of the status register: the condition code register.

4.3 The condition code register

The condition code register (ccr) contains five flags, Z N C V X, which are used to track the results of operations. Different verbs have different effects on the *ccr*; these effects are described in Chapter 11. But in general, this is what happens to them after almost every instruction:

* If the destination is zero, the Z flag is set
  - if not, the Z flag is clear
* If the destination is negative, the N flag is set
  - if not, the N flag is clear
* If there has been a carry or borrow during an operation the C flag is set
  - if not, the C flag is clear
* If the C flag is set, the X flag is set
  - if the C flag is clear, the X flag is clear
* If the high bit of an operand changes due to arithmetic overflow during an operation, the V flag is set
  - if not, the V flag is clear

By testing these flags we can tell what has happened as the result of a move, an arithmetical operation, a compare or a shift, and make our next move accordingly. The use of the ccr will become clearer when you learn the verbs bcc, dbcc, scc, comp and shf.

You must be aware at all times of how your verbs will affect the ccr. It is unwise to rely on the *ccr* remaining unchanged over the course of two or three instructions; put the instruction which affects the ccr and the test for this efffect right next to each other.

4.3.1 The carry bit

One of the first things you learn in arithmetic at school is about borrowing and carrying, and the MC68000 has facilities to mimic these actions. The status register contains 5 flags which play an active part in math. All the math opcodes affect these bits and your life is made a lot easier if you understand just how. You can't say that you know the math opcodes unless you can state with certainty how each affects the status bits. Let's look at the *add* family for some examples:

```
add #$a075, d0
   : d0 contains $7020
```

55

After the operation:

> : d0 contains $2095
> : C is 1
> : X is 1, because X=C
> : Z is 0
> : V is 1
> : N is 0

It is obvious that the result of the addition is too large to be held in the register so the flags are set accordingly. The result is not 0 and not negative. We can test these flags and branch on the results of the test using the bif opcodes, so the flags allow us to do multiple-precision arithmetic correctly. For example, add 2 numbers a and b, each 6 bytes long. Do this by:

> adding the first 2 bytes of each number
> adding the next 2 bytes, and the X flag
> adding the last 2 bytes, and the X flag
> if the X flag is set after this last addition the result is too long to hold in 6 bytes, so print a warning message.

This example can be used to illustrate these points:

> * a single flag is enough because in binary arithmetic a carry cannot be more than 1
> * 6 bytes .= 48 bits, a very large number, considerably more than 999,999 or 6 decimal digits.
> * there is a special add instruction for this manoeuvre:
> addx op1,op2
> :ops may be data registers or -ari .

Why this special form? A multibyte number will be held in memory in this form:

(6000)   b6:b5:b4:b3:b2:b1

(6006)   a6:a5:a4:a3:a2:a1

We want to add b1 and a1, then b2, a2 and X, b3, a3 and X, and so on. So if in this case An holds 6006 and Am holds 600C, it'll retrieve the right bytes in the right order.

The MC68000 provides binary-coded decimal arithmetic which saves some tedious conversion work. In bcd a byte holds two decimal digits, one in each four-bit nibble. Bcd arithmetic is performed a byte at a time, with results like this:

add 29,19 → 48: the carry is not set
add 99,09 → 08: the carry is set after this

Bcd arithmetic sets C according to the result, copies C to X, sets Z if the result is zero but leaves it unchanged otherwise, and does not affect V or N. These are called the bcd effects on the ccr.

The address modes allowed are *data register direct* and *-ari*. Why *-ari*? Again, numbers are usually stored from low to high locations with the least significant digit in high memory; but arithmetic is done in the other direction. If you use *-ari*, remember that the register must point initially to the byte beyond the least significant digit of the number.

There are three bcd verbs: abcd, nbcd, sbcd. All affect the ccr in the same way and use the same address modes.

4.4 Processor modes.

4.4.1 Supervisor mode

The MC68000 was designed for the demands modern systems would make on it. That means that it has to be a multi-user, multitasking machine. That in turn means that some part of the processor must maintain overall control of what all the users and tasks are doing. So the MC68000 can operate in two modes, supervisor mode and user mode.

What is the practical significance of this from the user's point of view? Some instructions are valid in supervisor mode but will be invalid in user mode. All these relate to the status of the machine. In user mode, any use of register a7 will address the user portion of that register. In supervisor mode, the supervisor portion will be accessed. There is absolutely no way that you can do otherwise. You can manipulate the system byte of the sr in supervisor mode, but not in user mode. The net result is that in supervisor mode only, not in user mode, you can do these things:

* set the trace bit

* set the level of the lowest priority interrupt which will be serviced

* switch to user mode

Once you're in user mode, it takes a catastrophe - or the end of a job - to get back to supervisor mode, e.g. r t e.

4.4.2 User mode

In user mode you can do anything you can do in supervisor mode except alter the supervisor byte on the condition code register or reset all the external devices on line at a particular instant. Most programmers prefer to write in supervisor mode, so that they can use all the commands available. Having written and debugged their code they can then set the processor to user mode before it actually runs the code at execution time, thus preventing the user from harming more than the part of the system they are dealing with.

SECTION 5
Moving Around

This section tells you how to use the verbs which move data around the computer, and the verbs which are used to direct program execution. These include some of the commonest verbs in the instruction set, and a couple of rare ones for completeness.

This section ends with an outline exercise, discussing the way in which we would use the verbs we have just learnt to perform a search in memory.

5.1 Moving data

In this section we will look at the way data is moved around the address space of the MC68000. The verbs we will look at are move, its derivatives movea, moveq; and its cousins movem and movep.

Many microprocessor instuction sets have a swarm of instructions for moving data. For example, there are commonly two verbs for getting data onto the stack and off again. There may be one instruction for moving data from a register to memory and another for moving it back again. The MC68000 gets away from all that by including a versatile and elegant move instruction.

move will transport anything to anywhere:

```
move (a5)+,(a6)+
move (a1),-(a7)
move (a7)+,(a1)
move d1,usp              ; a privileged instruction!
```

In various forms it can be used for address registers, multiple registers and data from peripherals:

```
movea.l $20,a5
movem (a5)+,a1-a3/a6
movep $16(a4),d2
```

move itself affects the condition codes, while move to *ccr* and move to *sr* can be used to initialize them explicitly. move usp is used to initialize the user stack pointe, or to save its value while other users access it.

The syntax of move is simple, as we have seen above:

```
move source, destination
```

The source for move may be anywhere; all address modes are valid. The destination may be any data addressing mode. An address register may be the destination, but then the verb is movea. The effects on the ccr are logic effects unless they are explicit - with *move to ccr, move to sr*. Operands may be word, byte or long.

Variations on move
There are two special forms of move, movea and moveq. The first is used to move data to an address register. Because in this case it is seldom desirable to change the *ccr*, movea will not affect the flags. Most assemblers can work out from the destination operand that you mean movea, so all you need to write is move. The operand in this case cannot be a byte - address registers don't handle them. All address modes are allowed for the source.

moveq is used when the source is a byte of immediate data. The data will be included in the instruction word at assembly time. The *ccr* is affected in the same way as by move itself. Some assemblers will be able to convert move with an immediate single-byte operand into a moveq, but don't count on it. The destination for moveq is always a data register.

move with *ari+* or *-ari* is an effective way of moving data from memory to an i/o buffer, or copying records. For instance, this sequence will copy 256 bytes from one location to another:

```
        move #$100-1,d1    ;initialize the counter
copy    move.b (a5)+,(a6)+ ;transfer the data
        dbra d1,copy       ;back to the beginning
        ....               ;task complete
```

dbra will be understood after reference to the section on conditional branching. This is the equivalent of a for-next loop using d1 as a loop counter. The combination of move and a suitable address mode makes the task extremely easy.

move can be used to load the *sr*, initialize the *usp*, store the contents of the *sr* on the stack or initialize the *ccr*.

```
* move data,sr       ;a privileged instruction
```

The source is any data address mode.
The *ccr* is set according to the contents of the source.
Operand length is word.

```
* move An,usp        ;another privileged instruction
* move usp,An        ;also privileged
```

Second operand is an address register.
Operand is long - the sp is 32 bits long.
The *ccr* is not affected.

This is the only way that the supervisor can affect *usp* explicitly: the supervisor cannot affect usp implicitly.

```
* move sr, destination    ;not a privileged
instruction
```

The destination is any data alterable address mode.
The *ccr* is not affected.
The operand is word.

```
* move data,ccr
```

The source is any data address mode.
The operand is word - only the low order byte is used.
The *ccr* reflects the source.

Note that there is a move to and a move from the *sr*, but there is no move from *ccr*: move from sr gives us this facility.

These special moves are not likely to concern you until you become involved in systems programming, and then you won't be able to do without them. Note that there is no move to the program counter - who needs it when we have *jmp* instead?

Block moves
There are two close relatives of move with their own special functions. These are movem and movep, which are used to move whole blocks of data.

movem is move multiple registers and is used to place a set of registers on any stack, or retrieve a stacked set of registers. This is of particular relevance in a multiuser environment when writing reentrant code. In order for an interrupted user to be able to retrieve intermediate results, the ccr and those registers used by the routine should be saved whenever the routine is entered. When the routine is exited, the saved registers are unsaved and the *ccr* is restored.

The syntax is as follows:

movem register list,memory
movem memory,register list

The register list is specified in the format:

register/register/register-register

For example, if you wish to save registers a1,a2,a3,a5,d1 and d3 on the stack, the register list is:

a1-a3/a5/d1/d3

You don't have to worry about the order in which you specify the registers - although it always pays to be methodical - because the assembler uses the register list supplied by you to set up a mask in the word following the instruction.

The assembler will usually allow you to define a list of frequently-used registers which you can use instead of reiterating the list each time you want it, so that you can write a command like this:

```
   move  rlist,-(a7)
or move  (a7)+,rlist
```

The destination of a movem-to-memory may be specified using one of the control addressing modes or predecrement. The source in memory for a movem-from-memory can be specified using one of the control addressing modes of postincrement. If you use *-ari* to store registers, you must of course use ari+ to retrieve them. This ensures that stacked registers are unstacked in the proper order and also makes movem compatible with normal stack usage. Operands may be word or long. For word-length movem-to-memory only the low 16 bits of the register are transferred. For movem-to-register, on the other hand, successive words are transferred to the registers and the fifteenth bit of each register is replicated to bits 16 to 31, i.e. the register is sign-extended.

movem has no effect on the condition codes.

Subroutines

In storing the status of the processor before executing a subroutine you are likely to want to save the condition codes too. This you can do by moving *ccr* to stack:

```
move  ccr,-(a7)
```

To retrieve the saved *ccr*, use *rtr* instead of *rts*. This will pull the saved *ccr* from the stack before retrieving the program counter.

To summarize, the function of movem in writing reentrant code for a subroutine you know is likely to be interrupted:

* make a note of those registers used in the subroutine
* on entry to the subroutine, save those registers - preferably on the stack using *-ari*
* save the ccr on the stack using move *ccr*
* before exiting from the routine, unsave the registers using *ari+*
* exit with *rtr* instead of *rts*.

rte restores the entire status register, so it does what rtr does and more. It is of course a privileged instruction - it alters the status register - and it doesn't make sense in an exception routine. However, you may want to make one of these reentrant too.

Routines for such things as disk handling are likely both to use a lot of registers and to be accessed by many users repeatedly. This is just the sort of routine you will want to make reentrant.

movep is used to transfer data between a data register and memory, and has been included to facilitate data transfer to 8-bit devices. It transfers bytes from the register to alternate locations in memory, or from alternate locations in memory to the register. The only addressing mode allowed is *ario*.

Let's take the example of a word transfer from d1 to a memory location given by $0220(a4):

movep d1,$0220(a4)

This is what happens:

* byte 0-7 is transferred from d1 to memory
* the internal memory location pointer is incremented by 2 but the address register is NOT incremented
* byte 8-15 is transferred to the new location

If the address given is even, the transfer takes place on the high-order half of the data bus and therefore the bytes transferred land up at even locations in memory. If the address is odd, on the other hand, the transfers take place on the low-order half of the data bus and thus land up at odd locations in memory.

This transfer can be reversed, thus:

movep $0220(a4),d1

Now alternate bytes from memory will be transferred to d1. The same rules about odd and even apply.

If the operand is long, the same thing happens but now 4 bytes are involved in the transfer rather than 2.

One operand is a data register. The other is always specified using *ario*.

movep has no effect on the condition codes.

5.2 Transfer of control

This section deals with transfer of control during a program. It therefore deals with those verbs which affect the program counter implicitly. These can be grouped into the pseuds: go; bcc; dbcc; comp.

This group of verbs allows the programmer to transfer control from one part of the program to another remote from it and, if necessary, come back again.

In the normal course of events, the processor increments the program counter after every instruction fetch and every fetch of immediate data or addresses, so that it is always pointing to the next instruction in sequence. This is fine in a lot of cases, but what happens when we want to go somewhere else for the next instruction?

5.2.1 When do we need to transfer?

There are three general classes of circumstance in which this happens:

* Something goes wrong and we take time off to fix it - this includes interrupts, which are not generally errors.
* Various sections share a common piece of code.
* The code we want already exists elsewhere.
* The result of a test changes the course of a routine.

The first case is covered by exception processing, and we deal with that in some detail in Section 9. Here we are interested in the last two cases.

In the growth of a systems environment, it usually (but not always) happens that there is enough cooperation within the department for a library of useful routines to be built up. This also happens within the development of single system, and is easily illustrated by reference to things like Unix system calls. These will for example handle input and output, given the right parameters, saving the programmer a lot of coding, testing and debugging.

If you know where a routine is, all you want to do is give the processor a clue as to its whereabouts and it will be able to find it for you. The clue it needs is either the whole address, or an offset from the current value of the program counter. Having given it a clue, you may go away and do the routine pointed at and never come back. If this

is the way you want it, that's okay. You can
achieve this by means of two members of the "go" family:

    jmp label1
        label1 is inserted into the program counter
or bra label2
        label2 is added to the program counter

jmp gives you access to the whole of memory and so you can use
it to access any co-resident code which has been inserted anywhere
at all. bra, on the other hand, will take you anywhere in the page
you're on at the time bra is executed. This is not to say that you can't
use jmp to get around the page you're on.

Having gone, you can't come back to where you left from except with
another jmp or bra, because the processor has no way of remembering
that you kicked off from a particular point. However, there is a simple
way of remembering your place, by means of a jsr or bsr. This puts
the address of the next instruction on the stack before loading the
program counter with the label to go to:

    jsr label1
        :pc → -(a7); label1→pc
or bsr label2
        :pc → -(a7); pc+label2→pc

Processing continues at the new address. Somwhat later on there will
be a single verb:

rts

This means 'get the long word at the top of the stack and put that
into the program counter'. This will send you back to the instruction
following the one which sent you away.

By the way, a subroutine is so called only because it ends in an rts
and as a matter of fact you can turn a whole system into a subroutine
by sticking an rts at the end of it and using a jsr or bsr to get
to it from somewhere else.

5.2.2 Why use subroutines?

These four commands - jmp, bra, jsr, bsr - seem to offer an
embarrassment of choice. Which do we use when, and why?

Consider first of all that we like to use top-down design and modular program structure. This implies that the highest-level or control modules will spend most of their time calling subroutines. This seems to indicate that we prefer jsr or bsr to jmp or bra and this is indeed the case. If you use bits of code in various locations and have to get back without relying on rts, you must keep track of your return address somehow. After trying flags and data locations you will arrive at the conclusion that the safest place to keep the return address is on the stack: which brings you right back to jsr and bsr.

Which do you use - jsr or bsr? If you write all your routines yourself, you are likely to prefer bsr in most cases, because all the code you need is conveniently located near you. In a multi-user, multitasking system with task swopping in and out of memory, you will find that programs written using bsr survive longer than those using jsr, because they are position independent.

This means that any code can be loaded anywhere in memory and will work, because all addressses are relative to the program counter. No matter whether you live in the top or the bottom of memory, your program will work because it is all fixed on the page around the program counter.

Against this we have to set the fact that many system routines will live at fixed locations in memory and so system calls will use a jsr rather than a bsr. This is no great problem because the environment is fixed and well defined in most cases. A jsr may take longer to execute than a bsr because it may have a long address rather than a word address - another point to bear in mind.

The "go" instructions - jmp and bra - are ways of effectively relinquishing control of your program and in a hierarchical system will not often be encountered. Once you go somewhere there is no guarantee you can get back. This is not much of a problem on small systems but on multiuser systems it can lead to embarrassment for you and other users, because your loose program may ricochet around. But here again, jmp is less desirable than bra, because bra preserves position independence and jmp may involve a long operand.

5.2.3 Simulating high-level constructions

Of course, in machine language there is no equivalent of the if...then...else and select constructions of high-level languages, so we have to implement them using - in most cases - short branches. The

69

select construction may be implemented using a branch (or jump) table. Short branches like these are usually easy to decipher or understand, and they are in any case unavoidable. It's the long jumps to outside our own program space which we want to avoid.

When you get to a subroutine, what do you do? A subroutine usually does something to some data you pass to it and passes its results back to you. This is known as parameter passing and we will deal with it in the section on module design.

We said that we may wish to depart from sequential processing because the code we want is resident elsewhere, or because we are diverted as the result of a test. How do we test in machine language?

This is where we discover the complexity of the bcc and dbcc verbs and their relationship with the condition codes, because conditional branching can be done only by testing. We cannot perform a direct test on an operand. Remember that there are five condition codes:

Z   is set for a zero operand
N   is set for a negative operand
C   indicates a carry has occurred
V   indicates an overflow has occurred
X   is a mirror of flag C, used in shift, rotate and math ops.

There are 14 different conditions to test for and so obviously we test for combinations of the condition codes, as well as the bare codes themselves.

We can test C, Z, V & N directly. To do so, substitute the "cc" in bcc or dbcc with one of the following pairs of letters:

CC: carry clear
CS: carry set
NE: zero clear (not equal)
EQ: zero set (equal)
VC: overflow clear
VS: overflow set
PL: negative set (plus)
MI: negative clear (minus)

For example beq would be used for "branch on equal" and so on. These are all straightforward enough. We can do them at any stage after arithmetic, logic or move operations. The mnemonics for zero and negative reflect the fact that we can compare two numbers and

70

set the flags as a result of the compare, as we shall see below. Notice that we do not test X. The prime use of this flag is in multiprecision arithmetic and in multiprecision shift and rotate operations. Since it reflects the state of the C flag, we test that instead.

We can test C and Z in combination; again, substitute for "cc"

    HI: C = Z = 0
    LS: C or Z = 1

This is relevant in comparing two numbers, which the computer does by subtracting one from the other. If the result is not zero and there has been no borrow, the number is obviously high. If there has been a borrow, the number is low. If there has been no borrow but the result is zero, the two numbers being compared are the same. This tests for:

    HI: a > b
    LS: a not > b

We can test N and V together:

    GE: N = V
    LT: N not = V

These test for:

    GE: a not < b
    LT: a < b

We can test N, V and Z together:

    GT: N = V and Z = 0
    LE: Z = 1 or N not = V

These test for:

    GT: a > b
    LE: a not > b

71

If a test is true, we branch to the offset specified as part of the instruction:

```
       "
       "
bgt  label 1
move (a5)+,(a6)+
       "
       "
       "
       "
```

If N = V and Z = 0, the program will take the branch to label 1 when it hits the bgt instruction. If these conditions are not met, it will continue with the move instruction following.

The only way that it can get back from the code after label1 to the move instruction (if that is required) is by means of a go (jmp or bra) of some sort. Then move must of course have a label. This is often inconvenient and many's the time that programmers have wished for a go-to-subroutine-if instruction. Perhaps Motorola will oblige in some forthcoming chip.

bcc is usually used as a backward goto - anathema to rabid structuralists but vital to effective machine-language programming. The sort of setup in which it comes into its own is this:

```
              "
xx            ;send characters to buffer until eol detected
              "
              "
              "
              "
              "
              "
       blt xx
              "
```

This will assemble into a short branch because it will probably take less than 256 bytes of code to implement. The label xx does not have to be particularly meaningful because it is merely a marker for the beginning of a block of code which ends with the same marker: it is unlikely to be used anywhere else.

The bcc instructions are matched by dbcc instructions which test the same conditions in the same way, but they have an added twist. dbcc includes a register which contains a count. This is the way it works:

The condition is tested.
If the condition is true:
    the next instruction is carried out
If the condition is not true:
    the register is decremented by 1
    If the register contains –1:
        the next instruction is carried out
    Otherwise:
        the branch is taken

In other words, the branch will be taken only if:

the condition is not true
and the register value is > –1

This is of course a loop with a loop counter and with a little ingenuity it can be made to perform all the functions of structured loops in high-level languages.

The sense of a dbcc is the reverse of the sense of a bcc. The bcc takes the branch when the condition is true, whereas the dbcc takes the branch when the condition is false, provided that there is a bit left in the counter.

Only the low 16 bits of the loop counter are used and the arithmetic is signed - otherwise how could you have a –1? So the maximum value that can go into the loop counter is 32k–1. Remember when you initialize the loop counter that it counts down to –1, not 0, so that the loop counter should be one less than the number of iterations you want.

dbcc will test all the conditions bcc will test, and two more besides: true and false. The first is equivalent to branch never, the second to branch always.

Let's see how to use dbcc to implement some high-level constructs.

DO WHILE

Here we need to continue with a loop as long as a specified condition holds. We also want to make sure - as is the convention with this loop - that if the condition is not true, the code in the loop is never executed. So we need to do two things:

* Select a suitable condition.
* Set the counter to 1 to start.

As soon as the condition is not true the counter becomes 0 and we take the branch. The code will look something like this:

```
        ...
xx      dbcc d1,label
        ...
        ...
        ...
        bra xx
label
        ...
```

If the condition is not met on the first pass, we skip straight to label, otherwise we execute the code at xx and then branch back to carry out the test again.

REPEAT UNTIL

We could write a block of code like this:

```
        ...
        bra xx
label
        ...
        ...
        ...
        ...
xx      dbcc label
        ...
```

Here we would branch to xx, test the condition, and carry out the code at label only if the condition were not met and the counter were not <0. Here we would set the counter to high values. If this were not enough, we could always interfere with the register during execution of the loop itself.

This particular implementation of REPEAT UNTIL allows us to skip the loop completely if the condition is met straight away, so that if the condition is true the first time the dbcc instruction is executed, the loop will never be done. This is not the way most REPEAT UNTIL loops are implemented, and so we may choose to leave out the bra xx instruction, in which case we get a loop which will be executed at least once.

FOR NEXT

```
   ...
       bra  label
xx
           ...
           ...
           ...
           ...
           ...
label
       dbcc  d1,xx
           ...
           ...
```

If in this case we choose a condition which will never be true, so that the counter is decremented on every pass through the loop and when at last the counter is exhausted, the instruction after dbcc will be carried out. Again, notice that the loop will not be executed at all if the counter starts off at zero. If we leave out bra label, the instruction will always be executed at least once.

A consequence of branching to a dbcc at the end of a loop is that the loop counter should be initialized to the number of iterations required, not one less as is the case when the dbcc stands at the head of a loop. (Do loops have heads?)

A FOR...NEXT...STEP loop with or without a negative step can be implemented with a little ingenuity. Like to try it as an exercise?

Branches assemble to one or two words, depending on the size of the offset. An offset less than 256 bytes is assembled into the instruction word itself. One of more than 255 bytes is inserted in the word following, and the offset field in the instruction word is set to zero. Bear this is mind when you bcc and bra: you may be able to save a word here and there by means of a little rearrangement.

75

It is worth remembering that you cannot branch to the instruction immediately after:

```
        "
        "
    bra nxt
nxt move #$3000,d1
        "
```

This results in a zero displacement for the branch. If there is a zero displacement in the instruction word, the processor assumes that the displacement is contained in the next word. And what the next word actually contains is a move instruction. So if this is added to the program counter, there is no telling where you will end up! Your assembler may be able to pick up this error; on the other hand, it may not, and your program will go wild in a way incomprehensible to you.

dbcc will always use two words, the second of which contains the branch offset. There is no space for placing a short branch in the instruction word because this word has to specify the register used as the loop counter.

It would be a little ironic if the branch instructions themselves affected the ccr. They don't.

As well as bcc and dbcc there is a third set of instructions using the condition codes. This is scc, which sets an operand to all 0s if the condition is true, all 1s if it is false. The syntax is:

```
scc byte
```

The 16 conditions used by dbcc are used by scc. The byte set may be specified using any address modes referring to alterable memory locations, except address register direct. (It would hardly make sense to set one byte of an address register to all 1s or all 0s!) The ccr is not affected by scc. Many high-level languages return −1 for logical TRUE, 0 for logical FALSE. scc shows why that should be so.

5.2.4 Comparisons

We can't use a conditional branch to its fullest without being able to compare. How do we do this? We use the pseud comp, which exists in the forms cmp, cmpa, cmpi and cmpm which refer to address registers, immediate data and memory.

76

How does comp work? It compares two operands by subtracting one from the other and setting the condition codes according to the result. Aha - these are the same condition codes as we use to decide where to go to.

Of course, if we compare two numbers a and b, we don't necessarily want to destroy either of them, and the MC68000 obliges by leaving the operands unchanged, altering only the condition codes. So in effect, comp tells you what would happen to the condition codes if a and b were used in a sub instruction.

The syntax for comp is:

comp a,b
    →set ccr according to b-a

a and b are unaffected. All the flags are set according to the result - except for X, which is unaffected. Remember that X is not involved in any of the bcc tests either. The different versions of comp are distinguished mainly by the addressing modes permitted for each.

    * `cmp` has its destination in a data register:
        `cmp data,dn`
    * `cmpa` has an address register as its destination:
        `cmpa data,an`
    * `cmpi` has any alterable location as its destination:
        `cmpi #data,data`
    * `cmpm` uses *ari+:*
        `cmpm (Am)+,(An)+`

Operands may be byte, word or long for all of these except cmpa, which does not deal in bytes. It is good programming practice to prevent anything coming between a comp and its branch, because you may overlook the effect some seemingly innocuous instruction may have on just the condition codes you want to test.

Source operands may in general be specified using any addressing mode - except in the case of cmpi, where of course the source is immediate data. Each of these forms of comp has its particular strengths and weaknessess. For example, to find the end of an ASCII string, we may look for a carriage return ($0d). `cmpi` will do this for us:

`cmpi.b #$0d,(a5)+`

This will look along a string until it finds a carriage return. If we *branch if equal*, we will branch if a carriage return is found. If we elect to branch if less or equal, we will branch on a carriage return but also on a form feed or even a bell. The second course may be more suitable in a word-processing application which allows both 'soft' and 'hard' carriage returns.

To compare two strings, cmpm may be far more useful. Let's assume that we are interested in a name filed in a record and are comparing it with a search key:

```
cmpm.b (a2)+,(a3)+
```

Here one string's address is held in a2, the other's in a3.

To look for all records before a certain date:

```
cmp $20(a5,d2),d1
```

Here d1 holds the cutoff date and we use arixo to locate a field in a record in a file so that we can find the date which (presumably) is held as a word of binary-coded decimal data.

Remember that we subtract the source from the destination, and the flags are set accordingly. The mnemonics therefore have the destination on the left and the source on the right. This is what I mean:

```
comp a,b      set ccr for b-a
bge label     if b>= a, branch to label
```

This is the only possible source of confusion in using comp. You don't have to remember which condition codes are affected, only that you are testing the relationship between two numbers and you need to remember which way the relationships go.

Now that you've been introduced to bcc, dbcc, scc and comp, you can see the utility of the *ccr* and will be able to use it to control your code effectively. Bear in mind that most instructions affect the condition codes, and you will very occasionally be able to drop a comp because its work has been done for you by some other instruction.

5.3 A keysearch.

A common requirement is the need to find an entry in a list given a few characters as a search key. There are numerous solutions for this kind of problem, but to keep it simple we will provide a simple specification.

We assume that there is a list of names held in memory, with a pointer to the start of each name in a table. Names may of course be in a mixture of upper and lower case, but we would like the search to be case indifferent: maca will match MacArthur or Macadam.

When an item is located it must be displayed so the user can confirm that this is the desired match. The list of names is not ordered in any way, so a search can continue until the end of the list.

This is a sample specification:

Get the search key from the user
If the search key is null, stop
Force the search key to lower-case
Repeat until the end of the list:
    retrieve a name from the list
    for each character in the search key:
        get the corresponding character in the name
        force it to lower-case
        compare the two
        if they do not match, exit this *for* loop
    display the name
    ask for confirmation
    if it is confirmed, exit this routine

We need these parameters:

* The start address of the pointer table
* The start address of the search key

Adjacent bytes are compared. Can we use cmpm? If we do, we will have to force the name in memory to lower-case. The user may not like this. Probably we will move the data to a register and use cmp. It would certainly be advantageous to look at four bytes at a time, taking care of cases where there are not four whole bytes for one of the registers by shifting the other one right.

Input/output routines will doubtless be available in the system library. All we have to do is find out how to call them when we need them.

How do we know how long each entry is?

We can make the first byte of each entry a length count or
We can subtract its pointer from that of the next entry

If we take the second course we are confronted with a dilemma in its precise classical sense:

How do we indicate the last entry?
How do we know the length of the last entry?

If we suggest that

(a) the end of the list is indicated by a pointer set to high (or low) values

and

(b) each entry be prefixed by a length byte, we avoid this dilemma - at the cost of an additional byte per entry.

In the C language, the problem is resolved by making every string terminate in a null byte. (hex 00). This has its pros & cons.

SECTION 6
Writing Subroutines

This section deals with the problems involved in writing subroutines, and tells you how to pass parameters safely. This provides a lead-in to the subject of reentrant and recursive code, which we illustrate with the well-known Sieve of Eratosthenes.

6.1 Subroutines.

6.2 Parameter passing.

6.1 Subroutines

A subroutine is a section of code with a defined function, specific inputs and specific outputs. Of course, this is true of a program or a system: but generally we try to make a subroutine a bite-size, easily-comprehensible piece of code.

A program which invokes subroutines to do its task may be slower and larger than a purpose-built program, but it will also be a lot easier for things we know we will do often, and so avoid reinventing the wheel. Once a subroutine is working it goes into our library and can be used again and again by any program needing it.

Subroutines don't just happen, although lots of them look as though they did. They have to be planned and documented. It's as well to do the planning and documentation in a logical fashion, and this is best achieved by having a fairly rigid system of writing them.

First, find a name for your subroutine. It should be clear, specific and unambiguous:

    sine
    taxcalc
    chequeprint

It should not be woolly, general and meaningless:

    findvalues
    prcessinput
    getbyte
    floogle

We've all gone through stages of inventing clever names which allude via Shakespeare and the Bhagavad Gita to the wife of the head of Systems, but we've also all been annoyed beyond belief at the use of such names by other jokers. Use names which say what the subroutine does. If the name is too general, so that anyone reading it would have to ask questions about it, it should be broken down into more than one subroutine. If the name is meaningless, it provides a snare for the understanding of maintenance or debugging hackers.

Once the subroutine has a name, write down precisely what it's expected to do in terms of its inputs, its outputs, any internal memory it needs and any constraints on data:

sine: accepts an angle in radian or degree measure. Returns the sine, using a Taylor series algorithm.

taxcalc: calculates the tax on a weekly salary, using tax tables on disk. Rejects negative salaries and amounts over $1500.

Include any remarks you think relevant:

> * This routine has been used by Sales for five years without complaint.
> * This routine works, but is very slow. If we ever find a programmer who knows any maths, we'll get him to rewrite it.

Now you know enough about your subroutine to begin figuring out how it should work. Try to avoid drawing flowcharts at this stage. A flowchart ties you down to a particular logic pattern before you're sure of the best solution. Write down the solution as you see it in minimal English - in which every word is a data name, a clear verb or the statement of a condition or a loop.

At this stage, you'll wish you had a pseudocode compiler or at least a high-level language to work in. Or that you'd taken up brain surgery as the easy option. However, you have to get down to it and work out how to make all the English words turn into assembly-language instructions. This takes a longish time, so start now.

When coding is finished, you have to assemble the subroutine, eliminate any compilation errors, and test your code. Testing is itself a science about which books have been written, but there are some rules to bear in mind - see section 10.3 .

6.2 Parameter passing.

Obviously, the more general a subroutine is, the more useful it is, within reasonable limits. Think of a block which turns all upper-class characters after the first in a field to lower-case characters:

GULBENKIAN ——→ Gulbenkian

This would be unduly restrictive if it were written so that the field length is always, say, 32. The way to avoid this kind of restriction is to pass the information it needs to do its job - in this case the field length - to the block as a parameter.

This kind of code is restrictive:

```
length equ 32
```

This is general:

```
move #length,d0
```

This is even more useful:

```
move #length,(a0)+
```

because in this case we can pass a list of parameters in successive memory locations simply by specifying the starting address of the first one.

This is useful, elegant and reentrant:

```
move #length,$12(a7)
```

because in this case we use the stack with an index to find our data. Any interrupting block will leave our data intact. When this block is allowed to resume its interrupted task, it finds its registers as it left them.

Parameters can be passed in a variety of ways:

* From input device (keyboard or file)
* In a fixed memory location
* In a register
* On the stack

Parameters passed on the stack can be retrieved at the start of a subroutine:

```
subr1
      movem1 $20(a7),rlist
```

Here we assume that the registers were saved earlier, before the subroutine was entered. Notice that we ask for an address which is obviously well inside the stack: remember that the stack grows downwards.

Parameters from an input device usually form a channel of communication with an outside system, and are therefore parameters which change slowly. In this category are things like tax rates, which may change only slowly but which we don't want to fix in program memory. We would be highly unlikely to use a file to pass parameters from within a program to a subroutine in the same program (although, probably, we've all done something like it as beginners!).

Parameters in fixed memory locations may be ideal: but they cannot be used for reentrant code. If we want to write reentrant code we must pass parameters in registers, or on the stack.

It is good programming practice to ensure that every subroutine has only one entry and one exit, and that this exit is an rtx. If you always do this, you'll find it easier to write reentrant and recursive subroutines. If you don't always do this, you subvert at least one of the principles on which the stack is based:

```
subr1     ...
          ...
          ...
      jmp labelx
          ...
      rts
```

If at some stage you leave subr1 via the jmp and never get back to the rts, there will be a loose address on top of the stack which you'll have to get rid of, either by adjusting the stack pointer, or by pulling the address off the stack with an otherwise redundant instruction. Keep your stack tidy - pull off what you put on, in last-on, first-off order. Another disadvantage of an untidy stack is that memory is not unlimited in any system and if you allow the stack to proliferate unpruned you may get a rude 'out of memory' message at some stage.

Remember that it's your responsibility to see that a subroutine ends with rtx, and that you get to a subroutine by means of a gsr. An rtx will haul a number off the stack and stick it into the program counter. If this number happens to be a telephone number or your bank balance, you're on your own. You may get an error message if you're trying to read from non-stack memory. That's lucky. It's far worse if the processor simply carries on at your bank balance, without telling you that anything is wrong.

The easiest way to wander unintentionally into a subroutine is this:

```
    ...
    ...
    ...
    bsr  subr1
    ...
    ...
    ...
    bsr  subr1
    ...
    ...
    ...
subr1
    ...
```

If the instruction immediately before the label does not halt processing or transfer control, you simply wander over the fence and into the subroutine, with unpredictable - but usually unpleasant - results. The answer, of course, is to put all your subroutines at the beginning of your program, and the subroutine driver at the end.

Let's look at a practical example of the sort of problem a stack can overcome. In BASIC, sqr(x) returns the square root of the number in the brackets. The details of how it does this are not important, but what is important is that it needs to keep track of x, the number of iterations it has gone through in getting towards the square root of x, and the intermediate value it has derived. Let's call the values it needs x, n and x'.

Now proga starts working out a square root. Along comes progb. If there were no stack, progb may think that the value of n it finds in memory indicates that x' is the result it wants, so it goes back and tells its user that the square root of 9 is 11. This may cause some doubts. proga carries on and comes up with a valid result for its own user.

On the other hand, progb may initialize all the variables correctly, carry out its job and take back the number 3, causing fewer scratched heads in its part of the universe. But proga may now do one of two things:

* It may find that its intermediate and initial values don't make sense the next time it tries an iteration, so it gives an error message.

* It may carry on and send back the wrong result, giving 3 as the square root of 123.

In either case, proga's user will begin to think odd things about computers in general and the one he is using in particular.

But look what happens when the stack is used to write reentrant code.

* Proga works on x, x' and n.
* Progb comes along and kicks x, x' and n onto the stack
* Progb works out its own value of x'
* Progb pulls x, x' and n from their locations in the stack before handing back to proga.
* Proga carries on, unaware that it has been interrupted, a program usually having less self-awareness than a turtle.

Reentrant code has a large number of uses. It would be silly to write a routine which does what the calling routine does, because it is unable to call itself. On the other hand, a routine which calls itself would be able to do so indefinitely, so it would be equally silly to write one which can only reenter itself a definite, small number of times because it overwrites its own data after a while.

Eratosthenes and Prime Numbers

As an example, let's look at the Sieve of Eratosthenes. This is a method of finding all the prime numbers in a certain region (of the integer continuum, not local government) by constructing all the composite numbers. All the numbers left over are prime. Let's say we ask for the prime numbers between 10^{310} and 10^{320}. (This is not something to undertake lightly on a microcomputer if you have anything else to do on it.) To construct all the composite numbers, you will need a set of prime numbers. How big are these prime numbers? Any composite number has at least one factor less than or equal to its square root, so the highest prime we need is sqr(10^{320}), which is 10^{160}.

Becoming reentrant ourselves, we reason as follows:

* We need all the primes up to 10^{80}
* We need all the primes up to 10^{40}
* We need all the primes up to 10^{20}
* We need all the primes up to 10^{10}
* We need all the primes up to 10^5
* We need all the primes up to $10^{2.5}$
* We need all the primes up to about 18

Light at the end of the tunnel! We actually have all the primes up to 3 at hand - quite literally - and we can use these to find the next set of primes we need, going up the ladder until we have the primes needed to access the region we're interested in.

Now all we need to do is program the Sieve, so we write the specification as follows:

* Call the region in which we are interested R, and its bounds B0 and B1.
* Call the highest prime we have on hand P. The upper bound of the region we can access with primes up to P is P(P+1)–1. Call this number P'.
* If B1 > P':
>   * Save B1 on the stack.
>   * Find the root of B1.
>   * Call this root B1.
* Repeat this process until we find B1 <= P'.
* Use the primes up to P to define the primes in the region between P and B1.
* B1 is now the new P. Pull the topmost B1 from the stack and repeat the process until we have examined the region R.

We can use this process to find all the primes we like and have time for, knowing only the primes 2 and 3 to start off with. You will have noticed that we build up to very large numbers very quickly.

90

SECTION 7
Register and Arithmetic Verbs

This section introduces you to the register and arithmetic verbs of the MC68000. It includes four exercises to familiarize you with the wrinkles of these verbs. After studying this section you should be able to use the MC68000 as a ready reckoner - which is a small step for a 16-bit micro, but a giant leap for a new programmer!

7.1 Using registers.

7.2 Converting ASCII to bcd and back again.

7.3 A bubble sort.

7.4 Arithmetic:
Binary-coded decimal
Binary arithmetic.

7.1 Using registers.

The verbs swap, lea, pea, ext, exg, adda, suba, movea are used to handle registers.

Two halves of a data register may be exchanged using the swap command, and the contents of two registers may be swapped using the exg command. (If this is confusing, tell me how you would have worded it?) ext is much less confusing. All it does is copy bit 7 to bits 8-15 of a data register for a word operand, or bit 15 to bits 16-31 for a long word operand.

```
swap d1
      bits 0-15 are swapped with bits 16-31
exg d1,a2
      the contents of d1 are placed in a2, those of a2 in d1
ext.w d1
      bit 7 is repeated in bits 8-15
ext.l d1
      bit 15 is repeated in bits 16-31
```

exg does not affect the condition codes. All the others cause logic effects in the *ccr*. Note that swap and ext are used for data registers only; all words ending in -a have address register operands; and exg will handle either.

lea is used to compute an effective address and load it into an address register for later use - as a parameter in a subroutine, say. This is particularly useful when you've just worked out how to find the clever bits of a data structure, and you don't want to forget:

```
lea $40(a4,d3),a5
      the address is computed and loaded into a5
```

This differs of course from:

```
move $40(a4,d3),a5
```

in that in this case a5 would end up not with an address but with the data at that address - hardly the same thing.

The operand is always long, and the condition codes are not affected. Control addressing modes are allowed. It may seem unfair to prevent you from loading an effective address from a data register. Don't worry:

you can use `movea.l` or `exg` (or is it `swap`?) instead, if this is your objective.

`lea` has a sibling, `pea`, which does the same sort of thing but places the result on the stack. All the remarks which apply to `lea` apply to `pea`.

`suba` and `adda` have an address register as their destination: the only restriction on the source is that it cannot be immediate data, so you cannot say:

`addi #1,a5`

but you can say

`addi #1,(a5)`

By now you will appreciate the distinction.

7.2 Converting ASCII to bcd and back again.

The ASCII string is located at (a5) and ends in a carriage return - $0d in hex. We'll assume that there is no other way it can end and that it is a reasonable length, but we will not assume that it is all numeric. If we get a non-numeric character in a string we chuck out the whole string.

What do we have to do?

* Look at each character
* If the character is a carriage return, we've finished.
* If not:

> if the character is not numeric, we've also finished
> if the character is numeric, convert it to bcd
> get its neighbour
> do the same with its neighbour - convert it to bcd
> combine the two to get a bcd byte
> store this byte and repeat

However, this method is a little easier:

* For each character:
> validate
* For the whole string:
> pack two bytes into one bcd byte

Let's see how we do this:

```
          lo.val    equ $30
          hi.val    equ $39
* ASCII 0=$30; ASCII 9=$39
          movea     a5,a6         you'll see why later
          subq      #1,a6            ditto
  nxt     cmpi.b    #$0d,(a5)     looking for a carriage return
                                  (hex 0d is dec 13 = ASCII
                                  carriage return)
          beq       packem        if so, on to the next stage
          cmpi.b    #lo.val,(a5)
          blt       reject
          cmpi.b    hi.val,(a5)
          bgt       reject
          subi.b    #lo.val,(a5)+ now the character is decimal
now a5 points to the next character
```

```
            bra        nxt
packem                                the string is okay now
a5 points to the carriage return at the end of the string
            clr        d1
            move.b     -(a5),d1        0000 aaaa in d1
            cmpa       a5,a6
which is why we set a6 to 1 less than a5's initial value
            beq        save
            move.b     -(a5),d2        0000 bbbb in d2
            lsl.b      #4,d2           bbbb 0000 in d2
            or.b       d2,d1           bbbb aaaa in d1
     save   move.b     d1,-(a1)
            cmpa       a5,a6
            bgt        packem
```

END

The result is that a number of ASCII characters have been packed into half as many bcd bytes. Of course, if there is an odd number of ASCII characters, the last byte packed has zeros in the high nibble.

Note the use of *ari+* to check the input string. A string is almost certain to run from low to high memory, so this is the form of addressing most suitable. On the other hand, when we packed the string we started from the end and used *-ari*. The first predecrement compensated for the last post-increment, which is part of the rationale for post-increment but pre-decrement: it avoids boundary clashes.

Note also that although it's not hard to remember that ASCII 48 is 0, and ASCII 57 is 9, it's a lot easier to remember the hexadecimal versions: $30 and $39 look more reasonable. Also we use names because it's easy enough to make a mistake. If we *had* made a mistake, we would have had to alter only an EQU statement.

We haven't written any code for reject: but this is part of the beauty of top-down, modular design. We can use whatever facility is available even if it's written by someone else. We can also insert a stub here to make the routine assemble correctly, so we can check the rest of the logic.

7.2.1 Converting BCD to ASCII

The converse problem is to convert a bcd number to ASCII. Here the setup will be a little different. The length of the bcd string should be known in advance: it's unlikely to have been entered from a keyboard with a carriage return after it! So let's say that we have the length of the string to be unpacked - in bytes, not characters - in d1, the start address in a5 and the address to which the ASCII characters will go in a6. The routine may look like this:

```
          subi      #1,d1           to get the counter right
nxt.byte  move.b    (a5)+,d0        aaaa bbbb in d0
          lsl       #4,d0           0000 aaaa bbbb 0000 in d0
          lsr.b     #4,d0           0000 aaaa 0000 bbbb in d0
          addi      #$3030,d0       add offset to 4 nibbles
          move      d0,(a6)+
          dbra      d1,nxt.byte
```

This is a lot simpler than working in the reverse direction.

The points you should note are:

* We use *ari+*: it would be awkward to go backward
* lsl (.w) followed by lsl.b changes d0 drastically
* We can see the offset in the addi instruction
* We have used d1 as a loop counter: this is a FOR...NEXT loop.

7.3 A bubble sort.

There are whole volumes dealing with the theory of sorting data into ordered arrays. Sort routines are often long, complicated and very involved. There is, however, a very simple form of sort called a bubble sort. (When I first discovered it, I called it a kick sort. Then I found someone else had invented it already so I defer to the conventional nomenclature.)

A bubble sort proceeds by comparing two adjacent items and swapping them if the first is greater than the second. Here 'is greater than' is taken to mean 'should come after'. Successive passes are made through the list of items to be sorted, until there is a pass in which no swaps are made. At that stage the sort is complete.

If all the items are the same - short - length we can compare them and swap the items themselves. With items which are long and/or of variable length, we compare the items but maintain a table of pointers. Instead of swapping the data around, we swap the pointers to the data.

If the data is to be output in sorted order, we use the ordered pointers to access each item as it is needed. If, on the other hand, the sorted data is to be stored, we may store the ordered pointer table and the unordered data.

Let's write a specification for a bubble sort:

        Set up a swap flag
        Let the number of items in the list be n
        Repeat until the swap flag is set:
            Set the swap flag
            Set p to n–2
            Set q to 1
            Repeat until p < 0:
                retrieve qth item from list
                retrieve q+1th item from list
                compare these two
                if the first is greater than the second:
                    swap these two items
                    reset the swap flag
                add 2 to q
        Output the sorted list

Why do we set the loop counter p to n–2? There are two reasons. We subtract 1 because of the characteristics of the loop counter. And we also subtract 1 because we want to compare the last pair, rather than try to access a data item outside the list.

Notice that we have not specified whether we want to swap pointers or data in our specification. This decision can be safely left to the programmer, unless the user dictates a preference. The implementation should be transparent to the user.

If the items to be compared are small enough to fit into registers we load them into two registers, use cmp to compare the registers and swap to exchange them if need be.

If, on the other hand, the items are too long, or of variable length, we load the pointers into registers. Then we use cmpm with ari+ to compare the two items in memory and still swap the registers if necessary. Assume that a register is large enough for the largest pointer; otherwise the bubble sort would last forever plus 10%.

7.4 Arithmetic: Binary-coded decimal arithmetic.

Hexadecimal arithmetic is fine for computers but not so hot for 10-fingered humans. The MC68000 recognizes our inadequacies and makes allowances by providing facilities for binary-coded decimal arithmetic. BCD arithmetic differs from hex in that a single byte will be used to store 2 decimal digits, rather than 2 hexadecimal digits: so the top value a byte can have is 99 instead of 255. This wastes a little space but is very convenient from a processing point of view, because there is no need for conversion between hex and decimal notation.

Of course, if the top value in a nibble is to be 9, the carry flag will be set as soon as 10 is reached, rather than at 16. The processor takes care of this automatically. If there were no bcd facility, you'd have to do this yourself.

Usually we store decimal numbers in memory with less significant digits at higher locations. Let's say we've got the numbers 2122 and 4048 at word locations 11 and 12:

Nibble	11	11+1	11+2	11+3
	2	1	2	2
Nibble	12	12+1	12+2	12+3
	4	0	4	8

Please note that we've calibrated in *nibbles*, not bytes. Each 4-digit bcd number takes 2 bytes or 1 word. Now to add these two numbers, we want to begin at higher locations and work our way down, adding from the right as we were taught at school. So we put 11+5 and 12+5 into registers - say a1 and a2 - and then we add up using predecrement:

```
abcd -(a1),-(a2)
```

We start at 11+5 rather than 11+3 because we're using *-ari* to point to the numbers. We can loop through this instruction as many times as we need to add two strings of bcd digits, giving ourselves multiprecision decimal arithmetic. The strings can be arbitrarily long, so there is no limit to the size of number we can manipulate.

abcd and sbcd both use predecrement, and both will include the X flag in their operations, so that any carry or borrow will be reflected in the next digit to be operated on. You cannot add single nibbles: this is a byte operation. There is also a bcd negate instruction, nbcd.

100

Remember when writing code using bcd that you should make provision for the case in which there is a carry after the last pair of digits has been operated on, for example in these two cases:

9123+   1025-
8095   and   2045

If you don't take care of this, you get entirely spurious results.

A small peculiarity to bear in mind is that the Z flag is cleared if the result is non-zero and unchanged otherwise. So if this doesn't suit you, you have to initialize the Z flag to 0 at the start of a bcd operation and check to see whether it's still 0 at the end. The other flags affected are C and Z. N and V are undefined after bcd operations.

Bear in mind that there's no bcd div and mul. You may add or subtract two bcd strings quite happily, and get good printable results. If you want to multiply them, though, you must do one of two things:

        convert to hex and then use mul or
        write a bcd multiply routine

These operations may also be performed on data registers:

abcd d1,d2

All the rules of memory-to-memory bcd arithmetic apply, and this is a byte operation only.

If we compare abcd and addx directly, we find this sort of thing happening:

(a1)=99; (a2)=11
abcd -(a1),-(a2)   addx -(a1),-(a2)
(a2)=10; X=1   (a2)=ba; X=0

An ASCII string in memory is suitable for neither abcd nor addx. To add two ASCII numeric strings together, this is what you have to do:

Pad the shorter string till they are of equal length
Starting from the right, convert the string to bcd, two bytes at a time
Use abcd to add the converted numbers
Convert the result to a suitable output format

Most high-level languages offer a choice of numeric formats. Commonest are:

2-byte signed integers
4-, 6- or 8- byte signed floating-point numbers

The signed integers are easy and quick to manipulate, being handled by means of addx and subx. Floating-point numbers, on the other hand, require a large amount of processing to convert from ASCII to the required internal representation. Once converted, simple addition and subtraction are complicated matters, although of course other manipulations are simplified by the conversion.

Taking advantage of these facts, you realise that things like loop counters in high-level languages are best implemented as integers, but numbers requiring extensive arithmetic manipulation are best stored as floating-point. This gives optimum speed and storage efficiency.

There are some high-level languages which allow 8-bit arithmetic, and of course this is faster than 16-bit for some computing operations. Those languages which oblige you to store every number in 6-byte floating-point format provide the worst of both worlds.

You have seen that addx is the hexadecimal equivalent of abcd. By the nature of hex arithmetic, addx can handle bytes, words or long words but in other respects is the same as its bcd brother. It also handles the Z flag in the same way, clearing it if the result is non-zero but leaving it unchanged otherwise.

Both abcd and addx allow either data register operations or memory operations with predecrement. This feature and the fact that they include the X flag in their deliberations indicates that they are specially designed for multiprecision operations.

7.4.1 sbcd and subx

Everything we've said about abcd and addx applies equally to sbcd and subx. In the case of these two, of course, the carry (and therefore the extend) flag is a borrow, but in other respects they behave identically, using the same addressing modes and the same operand lengths.

Both *add* and *sub* have an address register version which permits the manipulation of address registers without upsetting the flags. Look at these two examples:

102

Flags	Z C V X N	Z C V X N
Initially:	1 1 0 1 0	1 1 0 1 0
Finally:	0 0 0 0 0	1 1 0 1 0

```
add $20a4,d1        add $20a4,a1
```

Most assemblers will automatically convert add to an address register to adda. The operand may be word or long. If it's a word, bit 15 is copied to bits 16-31 - sign extension - before the addition is done. The effect of this on the unwary citizen could be a sudden leap from the bottom page to the top page of memory, so keep it in mind if you get unexpected results after an adda.

There is a suba corresponding exactly to adda.

7.4.2 Adding and subtracting in binary

add and *sub* will do arithmetic on binary numbers rather than BCD numbers. The bit pattern which converts to 0101 represents the number 101 in BCD but the number 257 in binary. The computer will handle both forms with nonchalance: all you need to do is be sure that you know what you want them to mean.

add and sub have immediate and quick forms. Due to a peculiarity of the nomenclature, immediate is slower than quick. addi will add the data immediately after the verb to the destination operand:

```
addi #$24a4,d1
```

Byte, word or long word operands may be used. An address register cannot be the destination.

Note the prefixed #$ here. # indicates that the following data is immediate rather than an address; $ that the data is in hexadecimal format.

All the condition codes are affected in the standard way.

The quick versions addq and subq differ from the immediate versions only in that the operand lies in the range 1 to 8 and is included in the verb at assembly time. You don't have to worry about these details and indeed your assembler should be able to work out where to use addi and addq when all you use is add.

addq and subq can take an address register as a destination and then they are no different from adda and suba, since they will not affect the condition codes either.

Although you may be confused by the plethora of *add* and *sub* instructions, the rules are fairly simple:

* *add* and *sub*:
  - use signed binary arithmetic
  - affect the condition codes in the standard way
  - use most addressing modes
  - may be converted by the assembler to
    addi addq adda
    subi subq suba
  - adda, suba do not affect the condition codes

* abcd, sbcd, addx, subx:
  - include the X flag
  - will clear Z if the result is non-zero, otherwise leave it unchanged
  - affect the other condition codes in the standard way
  - use data registers or -*ari*.
  - abcd, sbcd operate on bytes only, using bcd nibbles
  - addx, subx operate on bytes, words or long words

These rules tell you which form to use. Most commonly, you will use the bare *add* and *sub* with the appropriate length prefix, relying on addx and abcd for multiprecision arithmetic and letting the assembler take care of details such as the addition of a, q and i. I feel that it is easier to write i/o conversion modules and handle all internal arithmetic in binary, rather than use bcd; but you will no doubt have your own preferences.

7.4.3 Multiplying and Dividing

Arithmetic is not just a matter of adding and subtracting. The MC68000 allows multiply and divide as well, in two forms, signed and unsigned. To convince yourself that the two are different, just bear in mind that $ffff if unsigned represents the number 64k–1, while if signed it represents the number –1.

mul will take two 16-bit numbers and give you their 32-bit product. Since there is no chance of overflow, the overflow and carry flags are always cleared and the X flag unaffected. Z and N are set according to the result.

The destination is always a data register, so one of the two operands must be stored here to begin with. The source can be anything except an address register. Only the low 16 bits of the data register are used to derive the product: anything in the high 16 bits is ignored.

div is the converse of mul. Here the 16-bit source is divided into the 32-bit destination - which lives in a data register. The quotient goes into the low word of the data register, the remainder into the high 16 bits. If the operation is signed, the remainder has the same sign as the dividend.

Division by zero will cause a trap and hence initiate exception processing - which is why there are so many high-level languages which hang up when a zero dividend comes along. Overflow can occur easily enough, and if this is detected at any time during execution of the instruction, the V flag is set, the operation is abandoned and the destination remains unaltered.

Provided trap or overflow do not occur, the Z and N flags are set according to the results of the operation. C is always cleared and X is not affected.

Just what do we mean by trap? This is a form of exception processing initiated in response to an internally-generated error or an external interrupt.

When a trap occurs:
   * the *pc* and *sr* are saved
   * an exception vector number is calculated
   * this is used to get an address from the exception vector table in low memory
   * processing continues at this address until an 'rte'
   * the stored pc and sr are retrieved and processing resumes where it left off

There is more about traps in the section on exception processing.

mul and div, although convenient, take a lot of time. It is often more convenient, when using powers of 2, to do arithmetic or logical shifts:

```
0 1 1 0 1 1 0 1   two shift lefts:   1 0 1 1 0 1 0 0
0 1 1 0 1 1 0 1   one shift right:   0 0 1 1 0 1 1 0
```

The first case is obviously a multiply by 4, the second a divide by two. Provided you take care of situations where bits are lost, this is a faster method than `mul` or `div`.

7.4.4 More Arithmetic

Now that we can `add`, `sub`, `mul` and `div`, we might wonder how to implement other things - like floating-point arithmetic, roots and powers and transcendental functions. These can all be achieved using the procedures we know and love, although there are different algorithms with varying speed and memory requirements. There is a large amount of literature published on such algorithms. Altogether a neater way is to use a co-processor, now that hardware has become much cheaper. This amounts to giving your computer its own pocket calculator and saves you having to write the routines which do things like sin, cos and Fourier series.

As an example, here is how to produce a multiplication table using 2-byte abcd, showing the use of `dbcc` and *arit*.

On the back of every school exercise book I ever had, there was a multiplication table, along with tables of such arcane measurements as tuns, rods, poles, chains and fathoms. None of these meant anything to any of the pupils at the schools I went to: they were just a ritual form of decoration, like DIAL 100 FOR OPERATOR on public telephones.

The multiplication table was a grid whose cells contained the products of all the number pairs between 1,1 and 12,12. Having mastered these to some extent before I left school, I was astonished to hear that Hindu children learn the multiplication table of all pairs between 1/16,1/16 and 48,48. This doubtless has some bearing on the fact that Hindus invented so-called Arabic numerals. Although, to give them their due, the Arabs went on to invent algebra.

It is an odd fact about the multiplication table that it can be set up without multiplication: addition will suffice. Using this fact, we set up a multiplication table in bcd which will have room for the integral part of the Hindu multiplication table.

This may be done as follows:

106

* Reserve an array big enough for the table
* Fill each position in the array
* Display the table in a suitable format

To reserve an array big enough we make use of the RESERVE directive and let the assembler do the work:

```
table       RESERVE       48*48*2
```

The address associated with table will be the address of its first byte. This does no initialization. Why two bytes each? This allows storage of results up to 9999 using bcd - ample for our purposes. We could have gotten away with one-byte cells if we had been willing to restrict ourselves to results less than 255, as in the case of the non-Hindu multiplication table - but then we could not have used bcd arithmetic.

Filling each position in the array is not quite so simple. How do we do it? Each cell is the product of its row index and its column index. The first cell in each row contains the row index. Subsequent cells contain successive multiples of the index. So we need to:

> Determine the row number
> Zero the running total
> Repeat 48 times:
> > add the row number to the running total
> > insert this value in the next column

This is the inner loop: we have to repeat this for each of 48 rows as our outer loop. Let's look at the full spec:

> * Set up address registers pointing to:
> > start of table
> > running total
> * Initialize the row number held in a data register
> * For each of 48 rows:
> > Initialize the running total
> > Decrement the row number
> > Initialize the column number held in a data register
> > For each of 48 columns:
> > > decrement the column number
> > > add the row number to the running total
> > > move the running total to the next cell up in the row

There are those who maintain that this form of pseudocode is fine

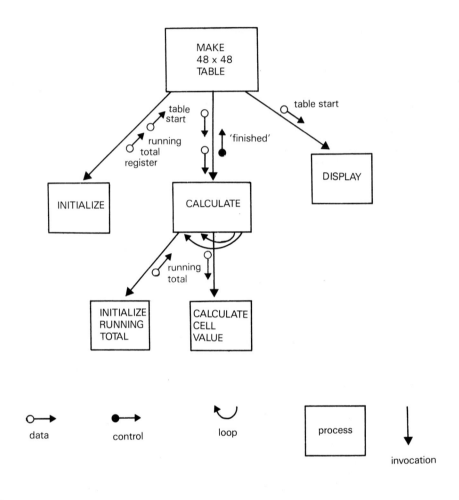

FIG. 7.1

A STRUCTURE CHART

for a multiplication table

for high-level languages but no so hot for machine code. Such people prefer to draw flowcharts. This specification is sufficient for an assembly machine language programmer, and has the benefit of lucidity. That can seldom be said of a flowchart.

It's handy nevertheless to have some diagrammatic representation of the process, and for this I have drawn a structure chart (Fig. 7. 1). Each block on the structure chart represents a defined block of code, be it a routine, a subroutine or just a couple of lines. The whole chart shows the hierarchy of the blocks - who's in charge and who does the work.

We have seen that we can implement a FOR...NEXT loop using dbcc at the head of the loop or at the end, whichever we prefer. Remember that the loop counter will be different in the two cases.

The same registers which hold the row and column counts can be used as the loop counter registers in dbcc instructions, because we are counting downwards. If we were counting upwards, we would have to make some other arrangement for the loop counter.

Arithmetic will be performed in bcd: this saves us the trouble of code conversion. In each case we have to add 4 bytes together. In many cases two and sometimes three bytes of one operand will be zero, but we have to do the addition to take care of the X flag in any case.

We use *ari+* to find successive cells in the table, thus avoiding the need for any kind of address calculation. This means that at no time will we actually be able to say immediately what cell we're at: but we won't need to.

The resulting table can be used for look-up and will be a lot faster to use than *mul*. In fact mathematical algorithms in computers often use look-up tables for faster running. It's obviously quicker to look up the square root of 9 than it is to calculate it: and I remember well an M6800 which used to tell me that the square root of 9 was 2.99999999 - after giving quite a lot of thought to the matter.

SECTION 8
Bit Level Operations

Here we deal with data at the bit level, rather than as strings or even bytes. We begin to gain a feel for the smallest elements making up our data, and an exercise on serial data transmission and parity checking reinforces this feel. For light relief we look at how to use bitwise operations to produce Arabic on a terminal; and we see how to pack 4 ASCII characters into 3 bytes.

8.1 Shifting and rotating

There are a number of verbs which involve the shifting of data in a bitwise fashion within a register or in memory. These are:

The *shift* verbs:
  arithmetic
    left
    right
  logical
    left
    right
The *rotate* verbs:
  rotate
    left
    right
  rotate with extend
    left
    right

We'll call all the shifts *shf* and all the rotates *rot* in this section. *rot* comes in two flavours, *rot* without x and *rox*.

shf and *rot* will move the bits in a register a given number of places to the left or to the right. This amounts of course to a multiply or a divide. With *shf*, zeros are shifted in to fill the spaces left behind.

There are two forms of *shf*, logical (*lsh*) and arithmetic (*ash*). Arithmetic shifts preserve the sign bit, logical do not. The "h" is, naturally replaced by "l" for left and "r" for right (e.g. asl, lsr)

There are two forms of *rot*. By itself *rot* does not use the X flag, whereas *rox* does.

shf and *rot* may both involve memory operands or register operands. If they involve memory, only 1 bit may be manipulated at a time. If they involve registers, up to 63 bits may be involved. The number of bits to manipulate - the shift counter - is then held in a register or follows immediately in memory.

Now let's look at *shf* and *rot* separately, in detail.

shf works like this:

* the end bit is shifted to the C and X flags
* all the other bits are shifted up
* a zero is moved in from the other end (except for *asr* - see below)
* the process is repeated shift count times

shf may be in any direction, so there are four *shf* verbs:

asl; asr; lsl; lsr

asl and lsl differ from each other in only one respect: if during asl the sign of the operand changes, the V bit will be set. The V bit is not affected by *lsl*. Look at these examples:

shf left 3 bits 01010101:

asl	10101000	lsl	10101000
	ZNCVX		ZNCVX
	00010		00000

You see that the result of the operation is the same in both cases. The three leftmost bits have been shifted out and zeros have been brought in from the right to replace them. This is the equivalent of an unsigned multiply by 8. During the operation the sign changed twice and so in the case of the arithmetic shift the V flag is set, but not in the case of the logical shift.

Whereas *asl* and *lsl* differ from each other in the way they treat the V flag without producing different results, asr and lsr may produce different results as well. This is because *asr* preserves the original sign of the operand. It is said to replicate the sign bit into the high bit of the operand:

shf right 3 bits 10101010:

asr	11010000	lsr	01010000
	ZNCVX		ZNCVX
	01111		00101

Not only are the condition codes markedly different in the two cases, the results are too, because of the replication of the sign bit in the case of *asr*.

shf and *rot* may use byte, word or long operands and may have a shift count of:

114

* 1 for a memory operand
* 1 - 8 for a register; the shift count is immediate
* 0 - 63 with both shift count and data in registers

An immediate shift count of 8 is held in the instruction word as zero. Your assembler may convert an immediate 8 to 0 as it should. On the other hand, it may not: you may need to experiment to find out what it does.

The syntax is:

> shf #b,dn
> :b is a number from 1 to 8
> shf dm,dn
> :dm may contain a number from 0 to 63
> shf memory
> :memory may be a direct address or ari/arix/arixo

Exactly the same syntax applies to *rot*.

shf has a variety of uses. For example, in data communications, a byte has to be padded with start and stop bits, or these bits have to be stripped from an incoming byte. *shf* is a reasonable way of performing the operation.

shf replaces bits shifted out with zeros shifted in, but *rot* will shift bits out one end and in the other. This is the way it works:

rotate 3 bits right, byte

10101110 →	11010101
ZNCVX	ZNCVX
00001	01101

C is set according to the last bit shifted out (and in again) and Z and N are set according to the result of the operation. V is always zero and X is not used. However, rox (rotate with extend) does use the X flag. The X flag is shifted to the receiving end, the bit shifted out is shifted into the X and C flags, and the process continues until the rotation is complete:

rotate with extend 3 bits right - X is set to start
and source contains 1100 1010; flags are:

```
        ZNCVX
        00101

0010    0100    1
1001    0010    0
0100    1001    0

        ZNCVX
        01000
```

This gives a different result from *rot* without X.

rot may be in either direction, and like *shf* may involve registers or memory, so that the syntax is the same as for *shf*:

> *rot #b,dn*
> b is a number from 1 to 8
> *rot dm,dn*
> dm is 0 to 63
> *rot memory*
> memory may be rotated in 1 bit only

Both rot and shf have a peculiarity in dealing with the carry flag, in that if the shift count in either case is zero, one of these things will happen:

> * *shf:* C is cleared for a shift count of zero
> * *rot* without X: C is cleared for a shift count of zero
> * *rox:* C is set to the value of X for a shift count of zero

8.2 Negation

The pseud *negg* comprises the family neg, negx, nbcd and not. These will yield the negative of their operand. The syntax is:

negg operand
    ← set operand to (0-operand)

negx and nbcd both involve the carry flag: this is subtracted from the result. nbcd is performed on bytes only: all the others may address bytes, words or long word operands. Any address mode except address register direct may be used.

The effect of a *negg* is to complement the operand and to set the condition codes according to the results. Because of the way computer arithmetic is done, negg is of course a way of multiplying by –1. not is a logical inversion, neg is a logical inversion followed by the addition of 1 (i.e. multiplication by –1)

negx and nbcd make suitable adjustments for 2's complement and bcd arithmetic respectively.

These operations affect the condition codes as follows:
    * nbcd causes bcd effects in the ccr
    * negx causes incx effects in the ccr
    * neg causes math effects in the ccr
    * not causes logic effects in the ccr

All *negg* verbs use the data alterable address modes.

8.3 Serial data transmission

Data from a computer may be sent to a peripheral device either in parallel or in serial format. In parallel data transfer, 8 bits are transferred simultaneously over 8 different lines, so a byte is sent as a single unit. In serial data transfer, each bit is sent separately down the same line.

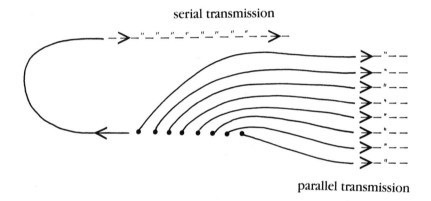

serial transmission

parallel transmission

When ASCII data is sent serially, it usually needs to have a little work done to it:

* Only 7 bits of each byte are sent
* A start bit is sent before, usually
* 2 stop bits are sent after, usually

So it takes 10 bits to transfer a single 7-bit ASCII character. (This is why baud/10 = cps.) That's still not the whole story, because the first of the two stop bits may depend on the previous 7 bits:

118

* If there is no parity checking, this bit is 1
* If there is parity checking:
    this bit is set to maintain parity
        - 1 if parity is even and there are an odd number of 1's in the byte
        - 1 if parity is odd and there are an even number of bits in the byte
        - 0 otherwise

Therefore data conversion for output involves these steps:

* set bit 7 to 1
* count the number of bits in the byte
* set the parity bit
* send the byte
* send the parity bit
* send a 1 to stop

Reception of an ASCII character is much easier:

* wait for the first bit
* collect the next 7 bits in a register
* get bits 9 and 10
* determine the parity of the byte
* compare this with the parity bit

Because only 7 bits are being transmitted, only ASCII data can be sent. This is a little tough if your files include binary numbers, so most devices will allow you to send 8-bit bytes, still framed by a start and two stop bits. In this case there are 11 bits per character and so there is a 10% increase in the number of bits which must be sent for each character, with a consequent but not commensurate reduction in the speed of data transfer.

What good is a parity bit? It's used as a check on the integrity of the data which has just been received. If the parity bit received by a device agrees with the parity bit calculated by a device, the chances are that the byte has been received intact. This is perhaps the simplest of a whole range of error-detecting strategies used in data communications. Parity checking is one of the functions of an asynchronous communications interface adapter or acia.

Our problem is to frame an 8-bit byte by the appropriate start and stop bits, allowing for even or odd parity as the customer requires.

How do we do this? The usual answer is, of course, "Hook up an acia" - but as a little intellectual exercise we'll do it by hand, as it were.

For each character:
Prepare for transfer:
Determine the parity
Set the parity bit appropriately
Repeat until okay from receiving device:
Transfer a start bit
Transfer the character
Transfer the parity bit
Transfer a stop bit
Wait for signal from receiving device

This specification makes no allowance for the situation where we never get an okay from the receiver - but that can be adjusted. It also does not tell us how to determine the parity. There are a number of different ways of doing this:

    * We can test each bit and count the 1s
    * We can use a look-up table
    * We can use a rotate

The first option looks a little clumsy. The code for it would look something like this:

```
loop btst d1,d0        ;test the next bit in d0
     bne  xx           ;if not zero, skip
     addq #1,d2        ;if zero, add to 1's count
xx   dbra d1,loop      ;repeat the loop
```

There would need to be suitable initialization as well. Somehow, this doesn't look elegant.

A look-up table sounds fine. There are only two problems involved:

Who sets up the table with no errors?
Do we have the space for it?

We certainly wouldn't set up the table we need by hand. We'd write a little routine which would do the job. This routine would end up being exactly the same routine as we would use to determine parity dynamically, with its output directed to the table rather than to a port.

120

How much room do we need for a table? We would need at least 256 bits - 8 long words. To find the appropriate bit we would divide the ASCII value by 8. The quotient would tell us which byte to look in, the remainder would tell us which bit of the byte was required. This bit would be sent unchanged for even parity, say, or its 1's complement transmitted for odd parity.

Division by 8 would be accomplished not by div but by lsr because this is quicker. The remainder would be determined in a similar way:

```
* clear a register
* repeat 3 times:
     asr the ASCII character
     asl the cleared register
```

At the end of this process the ASCII character has been divided by 8 and the previously cleared register contains the remainder. This is a fast way of finding the bit we want. We could save the 1 complement step by keeping two bit tables, one for even and one for odd parity. If we wanted something even faster we would simply use a 256-byte look-up table in which bit 7, say, of each byte represented the bit for odd parity,and bit 0 that for even parity. All we would do is find the byte using the value of the character to be transmitted and send the bit required. This would take more memory but it would be very fast.

The third option is to use a rotate. As each bit is rotated, it is reflected in the carry bit. We can use the carry bit to toggle a bit held elsewhere. After 8 rotations our byte is restored to its former state and our toggle bit reflects the parity of the byte. The initial setting of the bit we toggle would be determined by the parity required.

We would use just such a routine to set a table in the first place, and the amount of processing we need to do is not much more than the processing needed to access the bit table. This is probably the minimal solution. How would we set about coding it?

```
For each byte to be transferred:
     repeat 8 times:
          rotate 1 bit
          if the carry is set, toggle the parity bit
     send the start bit
     send the byte
     send the parity bit
```

send the stop bit

Notice that we do not stipulate the direction of rotation because it is irrelevant. This is easy to code and would give us a fast algorithm allowing large baud rates.

8.4 Logical operators

The verbs and, or and eor are logical or Boolean operators. It is strange that we come to them at this late stage, because they form the basis of everything a computer does - but that's a subject for another book entirely. Let's look at how they work.

Logical operators act on operands in a bitwise fashion:

7 6 5 4 3 2 1 0 of operand 1

7 6 5 4 3 2 1 0 of operand 2

The operation to be performed may be one of these:

* and: the result is 1 if both bits are 1, 0 otherwise
* or: the result is 1 if either bit is 1, 0 otherwise
* eor: the result is 1 if the bits are different, 0 otherwise

This is not the whole set of Boolean operators, but it is all we need for useful work. The usual way of using the logical operators is with a mask. For instance, we may wish to set all the letters in a string to upper-case ASCII, which differs from lower-case ASCII only in that bit 5 is always set. So we can set up a mask:

```
ucmask  equ %11011111
```

It makes sense to set up a mask in binary, because you can actually see what it looks like. Now if we did this using the and mask with all the characters in a string, storing the result at the spot from which the character was obtained, all the 5 bits will be 0 and so all the characters would be upper-case:

```
andi.b #ucmask,(a5)+
```

If (a5) were the letter a to start:

Bit number: 7 6 5 4 3 2 1 0

ucmask: 1 1 0 1 1 1 1 1

letter a: 0 1 1 0 0 0 0 1

result: 0 1 0 0 0 0 0 1

123

The result is the bit pattern for A.

Going in the other direction, we could have said that we wanted to change all upper-case letters to lower-case. Here we use or:

```
lcmask  equ  %00100000

        ori.b  #lcmask,(a5)+
```

Now any letter with bit 5 not set would have it set. All the other bits would remain unaltered.

There have been occasions when an ambitious terminal has swopped upper-case and lower-case, sending Motorola out as mOTOROLA. This can be rectified:

```
ulmask  equ  %00100000

        eori.b  #ulmask,(a5)+
```

Now any character with a 1 in bit 5 would have a zero inserted; any character with a zero in bit 5 would have a 1 inserted; and all other bits would remain the same.

Notice that ulmask is the same as lcmask, so that or and eor can be seen to produce dramatically different responses.

This is a fairly trivial application (although it can be used to keep undercapitalized correspondents happy) but there are other uses for the logical operators, not least of which is the manipulation of the status register.

How would you set the trace bit, without upsetting all the others? Answer:

```
trace  equ  %0010000000000000
ori  #trace,sr
```

This is of course a privileged instruction - you can't have users running around throwing the machine into chaos.

And how do you undo this state of affairs? Easy: using the same mask:

```
eori  #trace,sr
```

another privileged instruction.

The interrupt request levels are set in the same way, using masks and the logical operators. And when at last everything is as you want it, you can do this:

```
user equ %0111111111111111

andi #user,sr
```

This will reset the supervisor bit and leave all the others in their previous state. The supervisor state snores on until interrupted by an event of sufficiently high priority.

8.5 Bit manipulation

This section deals with the pseuds bit and test, which include the verbs btst, bchg,bclr, bset and tst, as respectively. We will also look at clr.

These are verbs that will operate on only a part - a given bit, say, or the high bit - of an operand, rather than on the whole operand. These verbs, by allowing us to address memory at the bit level rather than in larger units, optimize memory use and allow rather more elegant programming than is possible with byte-oriented instructions.

It is possible to look at a single bit in an operand and use the result for branching - or anything else you want to do. The verb we use is *bit*, which exists in these forms:

    * btst: test a bit
    * bchg: test a bit and toggle it
    * bcr: test a bit and clear it
    * bset: test a bit and set it

The word 'test' is perhaps a misnomer. What actually happens is that the bit addressed is shifted to the Z flag, so if the bit is 1, the Z flag is 1 after the operation: if the bit is 0, so is the Z flag. Then by testing the Z flag we can perform conditional branches. Remember that the Z flag is tested by the NE and EQ conditions.

The syntax of bit is:

bit number, operand

>   test (or change) bit number of operand

The bit number may be held in a data register, or be specified as immediate data. The destination operand may be any data-alterable location for most of these verbs. 'btst' is an exception: because it doesn't change anything, its destination may be any data location except immediate operands.

If the destination is in memory, the operand is byte length and the specified bit of this byte is addressed by the instruction. The operand is read, the specified bit is reflected in the Z flag and the bit changed, set, cleared or left unchanged before the operand is written back.

If the destination is a data register (it cannot be an address register) the operand is long. The bit specified is treated in the same way as in the case of a memory operand, but now you can specify any bit up to number 31.

Needless to say, flags other than Z are not affected by bit.

What is the use of bit? Obviously it can be used to handle 1-bit flags, giving large savings over the 8-bit flags usually needed in high-level languages - and adopted in low-level languages on those machines where it is difficult to alter a bit in memory directly. I have seen a rather clever implementation of the Sieve of Eratosthenes using bset to flag composite numbers. Of course, it runs rather faster than an equivalent program in Basic, and takes much less memory.

bit is particularly useful in various conversion exercises, where one code may differ from another only in the setting of a single bit. For example, upper- and lower-case ASCII letters differ from each other by one bit only: so to convert all upper-case to lower-case is a matter of setting a single bit.

bit has a relation which tests, not a single bit, but a whole byte. In this respect it is related to comp as well as bit. This verb, *test*, comes in two flavours, t s t and t a s. The syntax is:

test operand

This tests the operand specified by comparing it with zero. The result of the test is reflected in the N and Z flags of the ccr. The C and V flags are always cleared and the X flag is not affected: so this is like a comp in which the source operand is zero.

The two verbs differ in important respects. tas operates on bytes but tst will handle bytes, words and long words. Any data alterable addressing mode may be used.

t s t will test the operand and set Z and N according to the result without altering the operand, but tas will test the operand, set the flags as required and then set the high bit of the operand to 1: so the operand is always negative after a tas. This is not to say that the Z flag is always set after t a s, because its state depends on the previous sign of the operand.

t a s is an interesting instruction. It is the only one in the instruction set which uses a read-modify-write cycle. This is referred to as an

127

indivisible cycle in that it cannot be broken down into smaller steps. Because of this tas provides a means of communication between processors. A processor may perform a tas and the result can be read by another processor, without any danger of spurious results being generated as one process does one part of the tas and another the rest, i.e. semaphore operation.

If a bus error occurs during the execution of a tas, it is ignored until the tas is complete, to ensure processor integrity. In every other case a bus error would lead to the current instruction being aborted.

In spite of its importance, tas is not a privileged instruction. This is because it is quite conceivable that a user program could interact with an external processor: it is not necessary for the machine to be in supervisor mode to do so. Even more important, tas may be used for communication between different user processes.

clr is an instruction to clear an operand to zero and may affect byte, word or long word operands. The syntax is simply:

```
clr operand
```

Any addressing mode may be used. The condition codes are affected as follows:

* Z is set
* X is unaffected
* C, V and N are set to zero.

clr may be used to initialize large areas of memory, for instance on setting up an array:

```
move 256*4-1,d1 ;initialize counter
```

I use this expression to make my meaning perfectly clear:

```
xx      dbeq d1,label      ;test for completion
        clr.l (a2)+         ;clear 4 bytes
        bra xx             ;loop to beginning
label     "                ;task complete
          "
          "
```

This will set 1024 bytes to zero. dbeq is explained in the section on conditional branching. Of course, we could have achieved the same object by using move a zero operand but then we would either have had to set up that operand or use clr to zero the operand, whether held in a register or in memory. So clr is a neat solution. It's also faster.

clr will clear a block of memory dynamically at *run* time, unlike an assembler directive which clears a block at *assembly* time. In the case of the directive the block will start off clear but will change during program execution. In the case of clr, the contents of the block are undefined until the clr instruction has been executed. A lot of people come to grief because they forget to initialize memory. Don't allow yourself to be one of them!

8.6 An Arabic context processing terminal

The Arabic alphabet (the *alif-ba*) has 29 letters, all of which are regarded by Arab grammarians as consonants. These are written from right to left. Arabic numerals, on the other hand, are written from left to right - a hangover from Babylonian practices. This has affected the way we add and the way we write: we have to do our addition from the right, whereas we write from left to right.

If you are confused at this point, take a deep breath and read on. Although there are 29 letters in the Arabic alphabet, there are more than 29 alphabetic symbols in Arabic writing. Each letter may have up to 4 different forms:

* an independent or stand-alone form
* an initial form
* a medial form
* a final form

These are dictated by the position of the letter in a word. Those who know Greek or Hebrew will have a very faint inkling of this system, for in these languages there are letters which have different forms at the beginning and the end of a word.

There appear to be 116 different forms, but not every letter contains all four forms. In fact the majority have two: some have three and some have only one. You get different answers if you adhere to styles of writing other than naskhi, which is the usual form seen in Arabic books and newspapers.

But this simplification is offset by a complication. There are some combinations of characters which must have special representations of their own. Allowing for these swings and roundabouts, we arrive at a total of 92 different forms as a minimum for a readable Arabic character set. The problem then is to write a context processor which will select the appropriate form of a letter according to its context, and place that on the screen rather than the independent form which comes from the keyboard.

We are not interested in the problems of combining Arabic and Roman script, or putting special characters and numerals on the screen. All we are concerned with is to find the proper form of an Arabic character, given that character and its context - which is the preceding character.

An analysis of the problem tells us that the whole character set of a terminal capable of displaying Arabic and Roman numerals and special characters can be classified in two ways:

* finalizing or not
* modifiable or unmodifiable

When a character comes from the keyboard, this is what we do:

* If it is a finalizer:
    set the final flag
    look at the last character
    if this is modifiable:
        replace it by its final form

* Position the cursor for the new character

* If the new character is modifiable:
    if the final flag is set:
        reset it
        set the initial flag
    else:
        reset the initial flag
* Select and display the proper form of the new character

The combination of initial and final flags is enough to give us all we need to select the correct form of the required letter. This is best done by intelligent design of data. We assume that we have some way of distinguishing between Arabic and ordinary characters at the terminal end, so that by the time we get the character in our input buffer it can be easily identified as Arabic because, say, its value is greater than $7f. Let's assume also that all such characters are alpha only, not numerals or special characters.

We select the bit pattern of all such characters to be:

1 0 0 x x x x x

If we reflect the final flag in bit 6 and the initial flag in bit 5 using, say, bset, we have solved the entire problem elegantly. Now all we need to do is display the character represented by the new configuration either directly or - more probably - after referring to a look-up table.

We can arrange our character set so that all finalizers can be detected by a single compare, and all initializers likewise. So now we can begin planning our code:

```
initial     equ   (some value)
final       equ   (some other value)
```

To test for either:

```
cmp         initial,d0
cmp         final, d0          ;the incoming character is in d0

modify      equ   (some value)
```

To test for modifiability:

```
cmp modify,d1                  ;d1 holds the previous character
```

Let's try to put it all together.

What do we do with the previous character?

```
        cmp   modify,d1     ;is the old character modifiable?
        bls   xx            ;if not, don't bother
        cmp final,d0        ;is the new character a finalizer?
        bls   xx
        bset #fbit,d1        ;set the final bit
        move #1,iflag        ;set the initial flag
        bsr   output         ;display the finalized character


xx      ;now to deal with the new character


        cmp   modify,d0      ;is this a modifiable character?
        bls   xy             ;if not, don't bother
        tst   iflag          ;look at the initial flag
        beq   xy
        bset #ibit,d0        ;set the initial bit
        clr   iflag          ;clear the initial flag
xy      move d0,d1           ;new character becomes old
        bsr   curpos         ;position cursor
        bsr   output         ;display the character
```

This is the heart of a useful context processing routine. As you see, there are some unresolved problems, notably the stubs for cursor positioning and output. These will be highly application-oriented and there is little point in giving more flesh to them than we have done here.

8.7 Packing 4 characters into 3 bytes

There is a rather clever device on the market called the Organiser, a hand-held 8-bit micro from Psion Ltd which can contain up to 64kb of data on two removable proms. There are various data packs available with the Organiser, for applications like medicine, insurance and scientific uses.

Although 64k in one hand is impressive, it's a tight fit to get data into it, so to give the device more bits per byte the data in it is packed: 6 bits are used to present a single character. There is no lower-case; all characters are upper-case.

To turn data into upper-case packable characters, two things must be done:

> * Bit 5 must be cleared, giving upper-case only
> * 32 must be subtracted from the result

This gives 6-bit characters of which 4 are packed into 3 bytes so that 64k bytes will contain another 21k characters.

A lot of the development work for the Organiser is done on a development machine using the MC68000, so there is a routine available to perform the packing and unpacking on this machine. Let's look at it.

> * The data to be packed is shifted to a register using movep - register a5 contains an address 32 bytes below the start
> * Bit 5 of each byte is masked of using a data register containing the required mask
> * 32 is subtracted from each byte
> * The 4 characters resulting from this are packed into 3 bytes using logical shifts
> * The three packed bytes are moved back to memory

This is what the code looks like:

```
movep.l $20(a5),d1
```
d1 contains aaaaaaaa bbbbbbbb cccccccc dddddddd

```
and.l     d5,d1
```
d5 contains $df df df df - masking off bit 5 of each byte

```
      sub.l      d6,d1
d6 contains $20 20 20 20
Now d1 contains 00aaaaaa 00bbbbbb 00cccccc 00dddddd
      lsl.b      #2,d1      00aaaaaa 00bbbbbb 00cccccc dddddd00
      lsr        #2,d1      00aaaaaa 00bbbbbb 0000cccc ccdddddd
      swap       d1         0000cccc ccdddddd 00aaaaaa 00bbbbbb
- so we can access the byte containing 00bbbbbb
      lsr.b      #2,d1      0000cccc ccdddddd 00aaaaaa bbbbbb00
      lsl        #2,d1      0000cccc ccdddddd 0000aaaa aabbbbbb
- to replace the characters in the correct sequence
      swap       d1         0000aaaa aabbbbbb 0000cccc ccdddddd
      lsl        #4,d1      0000aaaa aabbbbbb ccccccdd dddd0000
      lsl.l      #4,d1      aaaaaabb bbbbcccc ccdddddd 00000000
      movep.l    d1,$20(a5)
```

Three packed bytes have replaced four unpacked bytes

Why did we do two swaps? Simply to move the third byte in the register to the first position, because we can manipulate byte 1 alone, bytes 1 and 2 together, or bytes 1,2,3,4 together: but we can't manipulate byte 3 alone.

This same operation takes about 30 instructions in 8-bit assembler, which gives some idea of the power and verstility of a 16-bit device.

Unpacking can be done by reversing these operations, taking care
      - to reverse the sense of movep
      - to ignore the and (we don't know the case of the original characters any more)
      - to replace the sub with an add

Note the style of commenting. Each comment shows us what is happening to the register: we can see the result of every instruction and thus verify our logic directly. This is especially important in a somewhat convoluted application like this.

SECTION 9
When Things go Wrong

Systems have been known to go wrong. This section tells you how the MC68000 handles things which go wrong and things to which it takes exception - such as out-of-range registers or division by zero. It also tells you what happens when an interrupt is recognised.

9.1 Exceptions, errors and interrupts.

9.2 Verbs for processing exceptions

9.1 Exceptions, errors and interrupts.

Exception processing refers to the way in which the processor handles the little problems that crop up from time to time in the life of any computer. Some of these are beyond its control: a power failure, for example. Some are due to errors arising when hardware fails. Some come about when programmers do silly things. And some arise when programmers try to avoid doing silly things.

The processor keeps a list of emergency numbers in a table called an exception vector table. This has 256 places giving space for 254 addresses. (The first number is the initial value of the stack pointer.) Each of these addresses points to the start of a routine for handling a particular type of error.

When an exception occurs:

The current status register and program counter are saved on the supervisor stack
The position of the exception address is determined
The address is retrieved from the vector table
The processor goes into supervisor mode
The trace is switched off if it was on
The exception address is loaded into the program counter
These instructions are carried out
When an rte is encountered:
    The status register and program counter are unsaved
    Processing continues where the problem occurred, with the
      T and S bits restored.

This process ensures that an exception does not require a halt or a system reset for recovery. This outline of exception processing holds true no matter what the cause of the exception. Let's look at the exception vector table in more detail.

The exception vector table resides at the bottom of memory at address 0-1023. The first four words are in the supervisor program space and the rest in the supervisor data space.

The systems programmer can alter any of the entries in the table so that exception handling is under full software control. This is useful to bear in mind if, for example, you would like some way of escaping from a crash on zero divide.

The first two long word locations contain the initial value of the supervisor stack pointer (ssp) and the program counter (pc). These values are loaded into ssp and pc whenever a system reset exception is executed. (This is not the same as the reset instruction, which simply brings external devices to a known state without affecting the processor itself. Perhaps we need another word here.)

The next three locations handle bus errors, address errors and illegal instructions.

A bus error is usually serious and presages incipient system failure, so the exception vector here should be to a routine that telephones your local service centre.

Address errors occur when the processor attempts to access an instruction, a word or a long operand at a non-even address. This is not allowed and will usually be taken care of by the assembler before it can happen. If it does happen, though, there is something wrong with your code that has to be fixed.

There is only one *illegal* instruction although there are plenty of unimplemented instructions. The only purpose I can discover for the illegal instruction is to test the integrity of the illegal instruction exception vector - a somewhat circular argument. A favourite occupation of micro enthusiasts is to write instructions using unimplemented codes and see what happens as a result. I haven't tried it with the MC68000 yet, although I keep promising myself that I will. There are ways of trapping unimplemented instructions and emulating them, which we'll go into later.

The next three vectors are for zero divide and the chk and trapv instructions. Here, as a part of normal processing, an exception will arise and the systems programmer will be expected to make intelligent provision for it.

Next there is an address for handling privilege violations. These can occur only when the processor in user mode attempts to execute privileged instructions. The problem is not the commands themselves but the mode in which they are executed. As far as I can see the problem of privilege violation arises in one of two ways:

  * An inexperienced programmer tries to do something he shouldn't.
  * A systems programmer falls down on the manipulation of the status register.

Either of these is a preventable cause of trouble.

There is a vector for the trace feature, detailing what is to happen when trace is enabled, followed by two vectors for unimplemented instruction codes - those ending in 1010 and 1111 respectively.

These latter allow you to emulate unimplemented instructions by writing code for them at the address given in the vector table. When the unimplemented instruction is detected, the system jumps to one of these locations and here you can sort out which instruction has caused the exception, and what sort of antics you would like it to perform. Perhaps you might like to write a routine which emulates a bsr-cc. Lots of us would find it useful.

Also, there are 7 interrupt vector addresses and 16 trap vector addresses, all of which are of more than passing interest to systems programmers.

When an auto-vectored interrupt occurs, the processor converts the interrupt level into a vector table address and loads the interrupt handler address from the vector table. Interrupt service routines end in rte, as do all other routines accessed through the exception vector table. An externally vectored table also exists.

Various peripherals or groups of peripherals are assigned to one of the 7 interrupt levels available. If there is more than one device associated with a given interrupt level, there must be some external means of determining which device has caused the interrupt, such as the supplying of a User-Vector.

During interrupt handling the interrupt mask is set to the value of the interrupt being handled,so that interrupts of the same or lower priority are disabled. Interrupt level 7 is an exception in that it cannot be masked: so level 7 corresponds with NMI on some other systems.

9.2 Verbs for processing exceptions

There are four verbs capable of initiating exception processing as a part of their normal execution. These are div, chk, trapv and trap in all its forms.

div initiates exception processing when the divisor is zero. The vector is number 5 in the exception vector table.

chk is an instruction which allows you to prevent over-enthusiastic users from reading beyond the end of a data structure or addressing something outside their allocated address space, e.g. in array bound checking. It looks like this:

chk data,dn

If dn<0: N is set and the chk vector is taken
If dn>data: N is cleared and the chk vector is taken
If the register is not <0 and not >data, nothing happens. The ccr is unaffected. The chk vector is entry 6 in the exception vector table.

trapv will check the overflow flag. If this is set, the exception vector at position 7 in the exception vector table is taken. If the overflow flag is not set, nothing happens and the ccr is unaffected.

There are 16 trap vectors located from position 32 onwards in the exception vector table. The syntax of trap is simple:

trap number
:0<=number<16

When this instruction is executed:
    * the pc is saved on the supervisor stack
    * the sr is saved on the supervisor stack
    * the address at location 32+(number in the table) is loaded into the pc

This can therefore be used for user or internal error trapping. On completion the processor returns to the instruction after the trap.

142

SECTION 10
Better By Design

There's more to writing programs than just learning to write instructions. This section tells you how to set about the planning which must be done before you write anything, and gives you an introduction to the concept of structured systems design.

The system is not complete until you've found all the bugs you can so we discuss the basics of testing; and then, because small is beautiful and faster is better, we talk about optimization.

10.1 Writing programs

10.2 Designing systems

10.3 Testing and debugging

10.4 Optimizing programs

10.1 Writing programs

Writing a program is not just a matter of finding a keyboard and banging away, even though this is the preferred method of many programmers who should know better. The programmer's task can be broken down into the following stages:

* Analysis
* Design
* Coding
* Testing
* Implementation
* Maintenance

These phases are diagrammed for you (Fig. 10.1). What happens at each stage is defined by its inputs and outputs. Unfortunately, things don't always work out this way. You don't always have a friendly - or even competent - analyst around. Sometimes the boss thinks that's all so simple it doesn't have to be done. "It's only a small program - why waste time analysing it?"

If you have to do everything, you often get people saying "Why aren't you writing programs instead of asking all these questions?" The pressure's on you to churn out code. Your first mistake is when you respond by churning out code.

A system which is designed at the keyboard is subject to the Programmer Productivity Law: the time to implementation is constant. Stated more simply, the system will always be ready next month.

To avoid this sort of problem, make sure that the part of the system development process for which you carry the can remains under your control. See that everything you need to do your job is there, going back to the beginning if need be.

Define the problem. Make sure that the person who tells you what's needed tells you everything unambiguously. Don't be afraid to ask questions, no matter how stupid they may seem to you, rather than make assumptions, no matter how trivial. If the user understood your business, you wouldn't be needed: if you understood his, you'd try to make money instead of spending your time programming. The user interface is the most complex in the whole system: make sure you get it right.

The definition of the problem is an unambiguous statement of the user's problems, but not of the solutions. The user may make suggestions about implementing the requirements. Brush off such suggestions as tactfully as you can. The problem is the user's; the solution is all yours. The problem definition should be in plain and simple English, with no omissions and no ambiguities.

The user tells you what must be done. Your job is now to work out how to do it. This may involve designing tables or data structures, or finding a mathematical tool which can handle the problem. When you define the method, you will often encounter questions about data ranges, boundary conditions and assumptions: ask the user for the answers.

Once you know how to solve the problem, you have to tell the computer. Now the matter becomes one of translating your solution into a series of steps the processor is able to carry out. Here you need to know that everything which should be in is included, and everything which should be out is excluded. You must also be thoroughly familiar with the language and the processor so that you can produce optimal code: code which takes up as little space and time as you can manage, yet is not abstruse.

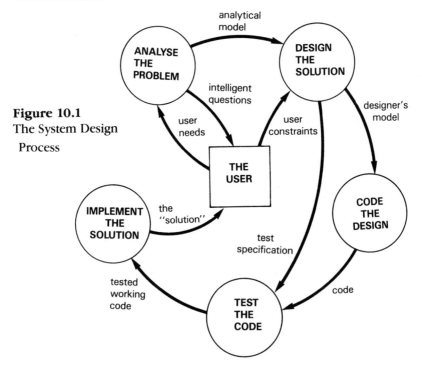

Figure 10.1
The System Design
Process

146

10.2 Designing systems

No-one learns a difficult foreign language without some ulterior motive - even if it's only to make it easier to get into bed with a native. The ulterior motive for which you are learning assembly code language is presumably so that you can 'write programs'. Anyone building a house is unlikely to begin without reference to a blueprint - although there are many structures which look as though they just happened, rather than were built. There are happenstance programs, too, and they can be spotted as easily as happenstance houses. So before you write a line of code, plan a little.

Software design has only become a subject for serious study in the last decade or so. Why this should be the case is a little obscure. The electronics engineers and physicists responsible for systems construction left the applications to people called 'programmers' - the ultimate dogsbodies of data processing. Programmers had only one task. They were expected to write programs. They were allowed to draw flowcharts, most of which were torn up, drawn again and torn up for good when the job was done. Those in charge also hoped that the programmers would document their efforts in some way, although they knew in their heart of hearts that the programmer would have moved on to some greener field long before the documentation hit their desk. The natural evolution of a program was assumed to be along these lines:

* Draw a flowchart
* Write some code
* Ask some questions
* Tear up the flowchart
* Write some more code
* Ask some more questions
* Draw a flowchart
* Repeat these stages until someone complains
* Run the program
* Test and debug
* Write some documentation

Woe betide the programmer who ignored this job brief. There was no way of measuring his work except by the amount of code he wrote, and it was pointless to argue with him about how good the code was, because you were working in the dark. He knew the jargon and you didn't. In the early seventies, people began to look at the way in which

147

programmers wrote programs. Their conclusion was by-and-large that programmers should spend more time on design, be more methodical about coding - and not write programs at all.

This conclusion may appear rather startling. Why should a programmer not write programs? Let's derive the conclusion for ourselves by discussing the tools which the clever - and often unintelligible - pioneers of systems design fashioned for us. These tools are:

Top-down, modular design
Structured models
Structured languages
Modular testing and implementation

What do we mean by top-down design? The idea is quite simple:

State your objective
Break up your objective into smaller tasks
Repeat for each smaller task
Continue the process as long as necesary

At each step we are closer to the final answer, so part of top-down design is stepwise refinement. This method leads towards a modular solution, but there is a lot of work to be done before we have the modules we need.

Let's look at a payroll application:

```
Task: print a payslip
- read figures
        read net salary
        read tax
            read updated gross to date
            read old gross to date
            read gross this period
                read hours this period
                read rate
            read free pay to date
            read tax paid to date
            calculate tax payable
        read NI contributions
```

148

```
- read form
     read employee details
     insert year-to-date figures as required by law
     insert administrative details
     perform coinage analysis
- write the payslip
- update the master record
```

We've shown the process to four or five levels: it's too exhausting to go much further. There is one thing wrong with this way of representing top-down design, though: it's too wordy. We need a diagrammatic method. A structure chart does the job; we'll come to that.

What do we mean by modular design? There are some things we do not mean. We never talk of modularizing programs. That's putting a loaded cart before a very tired horse. We define modules, then we code them. If a program has already been written it may be far less trouble to redesign it and do it again rather than 'modularize' it. We do not modularize with a pair of scissors.

What do we mean by a module? A module is a discrete, identifiable bit of code with defined inputs, defined outputs and a defined relationship between one and the other, like these:

* square-root takes input I and returns its square-root

* look-up-number takes input name and returns phone number

* send-reminder takes input name and amount-owing and produces output reminder-letter.

We can deduce certain characteristics of modules straight away:

We can't tell how a module does what it does from the outside. Does square-root use tables, an algorithm or an on-board calculator?
We can't tell how big a module is just by looking at it. It may be a keyword, a subroutine or a whole program.
Anyone who wants the output of a module should be able to get it by supplying the right inputs.

How do we isolate the modules in our system?

149

* Perform the top-down design
* Identify common operations e.g. square-root in 2 places:
  write the square root module once
  use it in both places
* Make the modules general - replace square-root and cube-root by find-root, which needs the root to be found as an input parameter
* Narrow the interfaces - make modules simple and coherent
* Some modules may need to be split
* Some modules may need to be combined

These rules are very general. Learning how and when to apply them is a matter of experience. If there was a set of mathematical transformations to design a program, you would be out of a job.

When you've identified all the modules, all you are left with is finding some way of implementing them. You do this by taking the fullest advantage of what your system has to offer by way of hardware, firmware accessible via system calls, other people's software from your user library, anything else that fits. What's left over, you write code for. As you can see, this method may result in a considerable saving of effort if you are working in an established environment. If not, you may find yourself with the rather thankless task of 'support programmer' - since you're doing that kind of thing 'anyway'.

The process by which a gleam in the eye of a user may be turned into a fully-documented, all-singing, all-dancing system free from 99% of household bugs is displayed for you in Fig. 10.1, which is a data map of the process. There are other parts to the model - we'll deal with them later. The point about the data map of this process and of another, superficially very different process is that both can be readily understood by almost anyone - anyone likely to be reading this book, at any rate.

Any system exists primarily to handle data - which is why computing is spoken of as data processing. But this statement is itself trivial, because we can think of just about anything as data processing. A cook in a kitchen is processing raw data - eggs and flour and sugar and milk - into a finished product - pancakes. The cook knows what to produce, what ingredients are needed and how to turn the ingredients into the product. This involves doing things in a certain ordered fashion. Cooks use models called recipes. Programmers should have a model as well, in addition to the programming model of the machine.

150

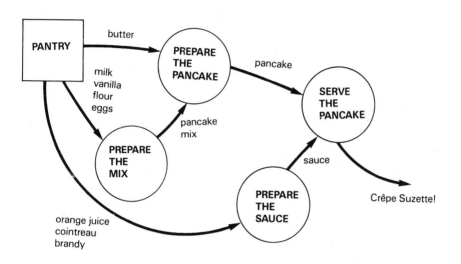

Figure 10.2 Data Map for Making Crepe Suzette

151

Since your systems will manipulate data, it's as well to have some way of showing the data entering and the data leaving, together with the processes transforming incoming data into outgoing data. A data map is such a model. Fig. 10.2 shows the data map a cook would use, if cooks made data maps for making pancakes. The model resembles that for the system design process because it uses the same symbols.

As you see, data is not adequately described on the data map, so there is a map reference in addition. This gives more information about the data in the system. It starts life very spare and taciturn, but gradually becomes more verbose as it passes through the hands of system designers and database designers, until by the time the programmer sees it, the data is described down to the bit level.

A data map shows what needs to be done to the data in the system but has no way of showing the order in which things are done. Since this is usually vital, it must be shown - and shown it is on a structure chart. We arrived at structure charts via the top-down design route earlier on. Here we see that they can also be derived from data maps. Fig. 10.3 is an example.

But a data map, map reference and structure chart are between them not enough to tell someone what the user wants, nor how to effect it. So we need to add a specification of the user's requirements in the form of do-whats, one for each process on the data map. A do-what tells us what the user wants done, and how it's done in the user's shop, but can't tell us how it'll be done in our system because it's our job to design the system.

These components - data map, map reference, do-whats and structure chart - form a model of the system which can be used by a programmer who knows how to effect the transformations required to write a program. It is incomplete, though, because this specialized knowledge is itself a part of the system model. We write it down on paper in the form of how-to specs, which tell the programmer how to convert input to output. A how-to specification is a technical document written by systems people for systems people, so it'll seldom if ever be seen by a user. Which is just as well, because it could scare him to death.

How-to's are written in various ways. The keyword is succinct. If an equation will do use it:

* $E = mc^2$

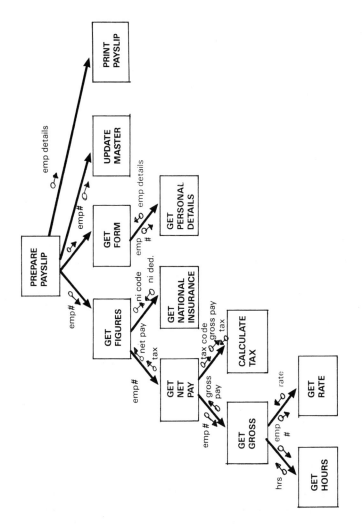

Figure 10.3 A structure chart for payslip preparation

153

If you need something a little wordier, you may try a look-up table:

```
*  J FM A  Y U  L G  S O N D
3129313031303131303131303131
```

If there is no way to avoid language, use a structured type of language like psuedocode:

```
For each employee:
  calculate grosstodate using grosstodate, hours, rate
  calculate freepay using taxcode, period
  taxable=grosstodate-freepay
  tax=taxable*.3
  taxdue=tax-taxtodate
  taxtodate <- tax
  return taxdue
  end
```

There are other ways of writing how-to's. If you bear in mind what the people who work with you are used to, you are likely to produce acceptable results.

There is another part of the model we haven't mentioned yet. This is the access diagram, which details the objects in the system and their relationships with each other. Objects are, roughly, files: but because database techniques move fast but the logical world more slowly, I avoid that term unless it's absolutely necessary.

The data map, data reference, structure chart, access diagram and how-to specs together form the progammer's structured model. This should contain all the information you need to write a suite of any required complexity. It is also the major part of the system documentation. You need to add little or nothing to it when inducting a maintenance programmer. All that remains to be written are instructions for the user. That's outside the scope of this book - why should I tell you how to do my job? You'll also need some comments in your code: but the modules are documented in the how-to's.

Notice that at no time have I spoken of writing a program. We've got down to the level of modules, and we write code for modules. Remember that a module can be anything from a system call to a whole new system, and a collection of modules can be anything from two system calls to a galaxy.

154

10.3 Testing and debugging

Your next job is to code and test your modules. Testing is often a hit-and-miss affair. Why this should be is a mystery. If you don't find the bugs, the user will: which means you'll get pulled out of someone's warm arms at night to fix them. To avoid this highly undesirable situation, make your testing exhaustive. Write a test plan which tests at least the following:

* Boundary conditions
* Zero
* Alpha and numeric data input
* Out-of-range input
* Timing requirements
* Overflow conditions
* Error reporting
* Error handling
* A range of normal input values
* Anything the user has found troublesome

If you don't find any bugs after this, you may have written a reasonably sterile system. On the other hand, you may have less imagination than your user. It's worth remembering that as fast as we come up with fool-proof systems, they come up with the latest in fools. Never credit your user with an unreasonable amount of competence.

When you've coded all your modules you have to fit them together and see that they can live together amicably. Now you will see the benefit of narrow, well-defined interfaces with as little data passing back and forth as possible, and of module independence. You may have to write harnesses to run lower modules, or stubs for higher ones. This activity contributes nothing to the system, but it is a necessary overhead, just like your food - which also contributes nothing except stains on the documentation.

If you are analyst, designer and programmer in one, you will need to develop the structured model yourself. This may seem like a waste of time to you and indeed sometimes it may be. But if ever you have to do anything of any complexity, or do something which you are going to have to modify later on, or something which someone else is going to have to maintain, or something for which documentation is required, this is the way to do it.

155

You'll notice that so far not a word has been said about flow charts. Everyone - including many who should know better - feels that a flow chart is the *sine qua non* of coding. This is not so. The structured design does not specifically include flow charts and yet can be used to represent very complex systems. Flow charts occasionally have a place in the how-to specs - but I try to avoid them and if ever I get into a situation where I find one unavoidable, I think again, very carefully. There are many reasons for my horror of flow charts, not the least of which is that their breeding, care and feeding is very time-consuming indeed.

10.4 Optimizing programs

Computers are more often used for their speed than for their infallibility, the latter being commensurate only with that of their users and keepers. They're also cheaper to feed than people, and in many cases take fewer days off, but that's another story. So, very often, we are asked whether we can make a program faster.

Now in the real world there are few cases in which even a sloppily-programmed MC68000 is not fast enough. It's simply that people are impressed by benchmarks which they dig up somewhere, or hearsay stories about other computers which do something similar, only very much faster: so we get asked to match these speed records.

One of the criticisms of structured program design is that it results in slower code. Of course, slow code that works is usually preferable to fast code that doesn't, and we use structured techniques because they deliver systems that work. But once we have a working system, there may be a valid reason for speeding it up. It's as well to bear in mind that it's easier to speed up a working program than it is to make a speedy program work.

What techniques are available for optimizing for speed? First, what's taking up the time? Every program has a number of different parts to it:

There is usually some kind of initialization
There are one or more loops
There are exit routines

Initialization and exit routines are only done once, while the loops are executed many, many times. Inner loops are of course executed much more frequently than outer loops. So start off by looking at your inner loops and move outwards from there.

What do you look for?

Think of a new algorithm. There may be a simpler way of doing the same thing. This is where a library - not a software library, but a collection of books - comes in useful. Read about the problem. Someone, somewhere, has come up with a neater answer. If the new algorithm gives you a satisfactory improvement, stop right there! You're not trying to break any records.

Look at the coding. Is there a neater way of saying the same thing? Are there things inside the loop which would be as well done outside? Can you move anything so that it's done as the result of a test already present, rather than all the time? If your modified coding gives a satisfactory improvement, stop!

Look at the code around the loop. Can a neater initialization speed it up? Could you enter it at another point? Repeat the process for outer loops, initialization and signoff, if you need to.

Look at the time spent waiting for peripherals, and the way those peripherals are handled. Disk access times, for example, are heavily dependent on the way data is written to the individual tracks.

Lastly, accept that there are some improvements you can't bring about. These lie in the hands of systems engineers, software engineers, even physicists. There is a theoretical lower limit to magnetic domain polarity switching, for instance, which limits disk read/write time. This limit does not apply to optical media. And there is little point in coupling an instantaneous device to something like Prestel.

An improvement in speed must often be paid for in increased demands on memory. The ramdisk provides a very simple illustration of this principle. A 10Mb ramdisk, though, is a little unlikely in the near future!

It may be desirable to save memory rather than time. This is in principle brought about by using an algorithm instead of a table. Memory is getting cheaper but the demands on it are getting larger, so for instance, everyone wants a personal computer that can set a 16-colour version of the Dow Jones index to music. It's hard to please customers like these, but we'll keep trying.

More important are those applications involving dedicated processors in large production runs. Here the cost of added memory is large in relation to initial programming costs, and the object is to get a complete medical diagnostic system, for example, onto a 2k ROM. The whole thing is then stuck onto a barometer bearing a drug company logo and handed out to new medical graduates as they leave the classroom for the last time. A 4k ROM costs twice as much as a 2k ROM and the drug company wants to keep its costs down, so you can make the system slow - although hardly as slow as a doctor - and memory-intensive.

There are some obvious ways of optimizing on memory:

* Replace j x x by b x x
* Replace abs . l by abs . s
* Use bytes, not words
* Use bits, not bytes

and some more subtle ways, such as using 3 asl instead of 5 asr to get a remainder modulo 32. Keep the stack tidy: reentrant code, especially, can make a stack grow like Jack's beanstalk. You can take out a table and put in a formula, or keep only that part of a table which actually gets used.

You'll probably end up with tight, incomprehensible, unmodifiable code. In these circumstances, that's okay - how much code goes into 2k anyway?

In general, the objectives of speed and tight memory are incompatible. The best way of chasing these twin objectives is to become an excellent programmer who knows the lanuage and the machine well and is in the habit of taking lots of baths - and so getting lots of time to think. I hope this book has helped you to achieve at least some those aims.

SECTION 11
Appendices

The first appendix in this section gives a complete list of the MC68000 instruction set, with a brief description of the function of each verb, its syntax, its effects on the condition code register and the address mode groups it uses.

The second appendix includes a discussion of the way in which various verbs affect the condition code register.

In the third appendix there is a table of address mode groups; and a table of groups with the verbs each is used by.

Appendix 11.1

This is a summary of instruction syntax, ccr effects and permitted address mode groups.

Where there are two or more closely-related verbs (such as *asl* and *asr*), their syntax is exemplified by a single pseud (e.g. *ash*).

The entries under *ccr* and *AM group* show the effects of the verb on the *ccr*, and the address mode groups permitted with the verbs. The entries are explained in detail in the section after this table. Note that some verbs are permitted different AM groups for source and destination. We use >*verb* to show source; *verb*> to show destination.

The line following each verb shows the syntax of that verb and the permitted lengths of the verb's operands. (B = Byte, W = Word, L = Long)

Verb	Meaning	Permitted Length	ccr	Address Mode Group
abcd	add decimal with extend `abcd dm,dn` `abcd -(am),-(an)` B		bcd	x
add	add `add all,dn` `add dn,alt` BWL		standard	>all;ma>
adda	add to address register `adda all,an` WL		none	all
addi	add immediate data `addi #,da` BWL		standard	da
addq	add 3-bit operand `addq #,alt` BWL		standard	all

163

Verb	Meaning	Permitted Length	ccr	Address Mode Group
addx	add with X flag `addx dm,dn` `addx -(am),-(an)` BWL		incx	x
and	logical and `and da,dn` `and dn,alt` BWL		logic	>data;ma>
andi	and immediate data `andi #,da` BWL		logic	da
andi ccr	destination is ccr `andi #,ccr` B		explicit	#
andi sr	destination is sr: privileged `andi #,sr` BW		explicit	#
asl	arithmetic shift left		shift	ma
asr	arithmetic shift right		shift	ma

(see note on pseuds, above)	`ash dm,dn`
	`ash #,dn`
	`ash ma` BWL			

bcc	branch on condition `bcc label` BW		none	#
bchg	bit test & change `bchg dn,da` `bchg #,da` BL		none	da
bclr	bit test & clear *see* bchg		none	da
bra	branch unconditionally `bra label` BW		none	da

Verb	Meaning	Permitted Length	ccr	Address Mode Group
bset	bit test/set *see* bchg		none	da
bsr	branch to subroutine *see* bra		none	#

btst	bit test
	 `btst dn,data`
	 `btst #,data`
		BL	none	data(1)

chk	check register in bounds		N(2)	data
clr	clear data `clr dalt`	BWL	–0100	da
cmp	compare `cmp all,dn`	BWL	comp	all
cmpa	compare address `cmpa all,an`	WL	comp	all
cmpi	compare immediate `cmpi #,da`	BWL	comp	all
cmpm	compare memory `cmpm (am)+,(an)+`	BWL	comp	ari+
dbcc	test, decrement & branch `dbcc dn,label`	W	none	D,label
divs divu	divide signed divide unsigned `div data,dn`	 W	div div	data data
eor	exclusive or `eor dn,da`	BWL	logic	da

Verb	Meaning	Permitted Length	ccr	Address Mode Group
eori	eor with immediate data eori #,da	BWL	logic	da
eori ccr	destination is ccr eori #,ccr	B	explicit	#
eori sr	destination is sr: privileged eori #,sr	W	explicit	#
exg	exchange registers exg r1,r2	L	none	A an D registers
ext	extend sign ext dn	WL	logic	Data registers
illegal	(causes illegal exception) illegal		none	–
jmp	jump unconditionally		none	control
jsr	jump label; jump to subroutine jsr label		none	control
lea	load effective address into A lea control,an	L	none	control
link	use register as stack pointer link an,#		none	A,#

Verb	Meaning	Permitted Length	ccr	Address Mode Group
lsl	logical shift left		lshift	ma
lsr	logical shift right lsh dm,dn lsh #,dn lsh ma	BW	lshift	ma
move	transfer data move all,da	BWL	logic	>all;da>
move ccr	ccr is destination move data,ccr	B	explicit	data
move sr	sr is source move sr,da	W	none	da
move sr	sr is destination: privileged move data,sr	W	explicit	data

move usp	move to/from usp:
	privileged
	move usp,da
	move data,usp
		WL	none
			
			data
				da

movea	move to address register movea all,an	WL	none	all
movem	move registers to memory movem register list, control	WL	none	control with −ari
movem	move memory to registers movem control, register list	WL	none	control with ari+

Verb	Meaning	Permitted Length	ccr	Address Mode Group
`movep`	move registers to alt bytes `movem d,o(an)`	WL	none	D,ario
`movep`	move alt bytes to register `movep o(an),d`	WL	none	ario,D
`moveq`	move 8-bit immediate data `moveq #,dn`	L	logic	#,D
`muls` `mulu`	multiply signed multiply unsigned `mul data,dn`	W	logic logic	data data
`nbcd`	negate bcd with X `nbcd da`	B	bcd	da
`neg` `negx`	negate without X negate with X `negg da`	BWL	standard incx	da x
`nop`	no operation `nop`		none	none
`not`	form one's complement `not da`	BWL	logic	da
`or`	logical or `or data,dn` `or dn,ma`	BWL	logic	>data;ma>
`ori`	or immediate data `ori #,dalt`	BWL	logic	da
`ori ccr`	ccr is destination `ori #,ccr`	B	explicit	#

Verb	Meaning	Permitted Length	ccr	Address Mode Group
`ori sr`	sr is destination: privileged `ori #,sr` — W		explicit	#
`pea`	push effective address to stack `pea control` — L		none	control
`reset`	reset external devices `reset`		none	none
`rol`	rotate left		rot	ma
`ror`	rotate right		rot	ma
`roxl`	rotate left with extend		rox	ma
`roxr`	rotate right with extend `rot dm,dn` `rot #,dn` `rot ma` — BWL		rox	ma
`rte`	return from exception: privileged		implicit	–
`rtr`	return & restore ccr		implicit	–
`rts`	return from subroutine `rtx`		none	–
`sbcd`	subtract decimal with extend `sbcd dm,dn` `sbcd -(am),-(an)` — B		bcd	x
`scc`	set on condition `scc da` — B		none	da

169

Verb	Meaning	Permitted Length	ccr	Address Mode Group
stop	stop program and load sr stop #	 W	explicit	#

sub	subtract
	sub all,dn
	sub dn,alt
		
		BWL
			standard	>all
				ma

suba	subtract from address register suba all,an	 WL	none	all
subi	subtract immediate data subi #,da	 BWL	standard	da
subq	subtract 3-bit data subq #,alt	 BWL	standard	alt

subx	subtract with X
	subx dm,dn
	subx -(am),-(an)
		
		BWL
			incx	x

swap swap dn	swap register halves W		logic	D
tas	test and set - indivisible tas da	 B	logic	da
trap	jump to trap routine trap #		none	#
trapv	trap on overflow trapv		none	–

Verb	Meaning	Permitted Length	ccr	Address Mode Group
tst	compare with zero tst da	BWL	logic	da
unlk	restore stack pointer unlk		none	A

Appendix 11.2 Interpreting the ccr entries

The following section tells you how to interpret the entry under ccr in the verb table.

Implicit effects on the ccr come about when the ccr is reloaded from the stack. This occurs with rte and rtr.

Explicit effects occur with those verbs which address the ccr directly - such as move to sr, andi to sr.

bcd effects occur with abcd, nbcd and sbcd:

* Z is set for zero, unchanged otherwise
* C is set for carry, cleared otherwise
* X is set the same as the carry bit
* N and V are undefined

incx effects occur with verbs which include the X flag in their operations - addx, subx, negx:

* Z is set for zero, unchanged otherwise
* N is set for negative, cleared otherwise
* C is set for carry, cleared otherwise
* X is set the same as C
* V is set if overflow occurs, cleared otherwise

Note that overflow occurs if the most significant bit of an operand changes during execution of the instruction and usually indicates that the destination field is not large enough to hold the result. For multiprecision arithmetic it is usual to clear the Z flag at the start of the instruction sequence, and test for a zero result at the end. You see that bcd and incx treat the Z flag in the same way.

The standard effects occur with many verbs:

* Z is set for zero, cleared otherwise
* N is set for zero, cleared otherwise
* C is set for a carry, cleared otherwise
* X reflects C
* V is set if overflow occurs, cleared otherwise.

These differ from incx effects only in the treatment of the Z flag.

Logic effects occur with and, or, not, move and some others:

* Z is set for zero, cleared otherwise
* N is set for negative, cleared otherwise
* C and V are always cleared
* X is unaffected

It is obvious that if the destination of a logical operation is the ccr, the contents of the ccr will depend entirely on the source operand, not on these rules!

The shift effects appear with asl, asr:

* N is set if the result is negative, cleared otherwise
* Z is set for zero, cleared otherwise
* V is set if the msb changes during the operation
* C is set according to the last bit shifted out
  - but C is cleared for a shift count of 0
* X reflects C - but is unchanged by a shift count of 0

The rox effects appear with roxl, roxr:

* N is set for negative, cleared otherwise
* Z is set for zero, cleared otherwise
* V is always cleared
* C is set according to the last bit shifted out
  - but C reflects X for a shift count of 0
* X reflects C - but X is not affected for a shift count of 0

The rot effects appear with rol, ror:

* N is set for negative, cleared otherwise
* Z is set for zero, cleared otherwise
* C reflects the last bit shifted - and is cleared for a shift count of zero
* V is always cleared
* X is not affected

The lshift effects appear with logical shifts:

173

* N is set for negative, cleared otherwise
* Z is set for zero, cleared otherwise
* V is always cleared
* C is set according to the last bit shifted out
  - but C is cleared for a shift count of 0
* X reflects C - but X is unaffected for a shift count of 0

The differences between `shift`, `lshift`, `rox` and `rot` effects can be summed up thus:

* `shift` affects V arithmetically
* `lshift` and `rot` clear V
* `shift` and `lshift` clear C and leave V unchanged for a shift count of 0
* `rot` does not affect X, and clears C for a shift count of 0
* `rox` clears X and leaves C unchanged for a shift count of 0

In all other respects, the effects of these verbs on the ccr are standard.

Appendix 11.3 Address Mode Groups

Mode	1	2	3	4	5	6	7	8
A register	*		*					
D register	*	*	*	*				
-ari	*	*	*	*	*		*	
ari+	*	*	*	*	*			
ari	*	*	*	*	*	*		
ario	*	*	*	*	*	*		
arixo	*	*	*	*	*	*		
abs.s	*	*	*	*	*	*		
abs.l	*	*	*	*	*	*		
pcro	*	*				*		
pcrox	*	*				*		
imm	*	*						*

Groups are called:
1: all
2: data
3: alterable (al)
4: data alterable (da)
5: memory alterable (ma)
6: control
7: x - flag
8: #

Address mode group	Verbs using these groups
all	>add, adda, cmp, cmpa, >move, movea, >sub, suba
data	>and, btst(1), chk, divs, divu, move to ccr, move to sr, muls, mulu, >or
alterable (alt)	addq, subq
data alterable (da)	addi, andi, bchg, bclr, bset, clr, cmpi, eor, eori, move>, move from sr, nbcd, neg, negx, not, ori, scc, subi, tas, tst
memory alterable (ma)	add>, and>, asl, asr, lsl, lsr, or> rol, ror, roxl, roxr, sub>
control	jmp, jsr, lea, >movem(2), movem>(3), pea
x flag (x)	abcd, sbcd, addx, subx
#	andi, bcc, bsr, eori, link, moveq, ori, stop, trap

(Read >verb as 'source operand for verb';
verb> as 'destination operand for verb'.)

(1) b t s t cannot use immediate addressing
(2) >movem may be *ari+* in addition to control
(3) movem> may be *–ari* as well as control

N.B. (2),(3): movem may not use p c r o or p c r o x

INDEX